Complexes

Complexes

Diagnosis and Therapy
in Analytical Psychology

HANS DIECKMANN

Translated by
BORIS MATTHEWS

Chiron Publications
Wilmette, IL

Originally published in 1991 as *Komplexe : Diagnostik und Therapie in der analytischen Psychologie*
© 1991 Springer-Verlag, Berlin.

Library of Congress Catalog Card Number: 98-56173

Printed in the United States of America.
Cover design by D. J. Hyde.

Library of Congress Catalog-in-Publication Data:
 Dieckmann, Hans.
  [Komplexe. English]
  Complexes : diagnosis and therapy in analytical psychology / Hans Dieckmann ; translated by Boris Matthews.
    p.   cm.
  Includes bibliographical references.
  ISBN 1-888602-09-0 (alk. paper)
  1. Complexes (Psychology) 2. Jungian psychology. I. Title.
 RC569.5.C68D5413 1999
 616.89--dc21   98-56173
                                                           CIP

Contents

Introduction

Complexes have been known and described in all cultures, past and present, although they have not been so designated. Primal peoples, who obviously succumb more easily to psychic dissociation, have always known of possession by spirits, demons, or even gods. These forces, as a second personality, usurp the position of the ego-complex and are the cause of affects and actions that are actually foreign to the normal personality of the affected person. As Eliade (1964) has described, shamanism in large part consists of removing the foreign emotional component from the body or the soul of the person afflicted in this way. In contemporary language, we would call it releasing the ego-complex from identification with, or inflation by, the complex and repressing the latter back into the unconscious. In the case of the so-called "loss of soul," that is, an extensive unconsciousness of the ego, the shaman undertakes a journey into either the upper or the lower world in order to recover the lost soul. Lévy-Bruhl (1923) portrays the extent to which primal peoples believe foreign "souls" are able to invade one's own psyche:

> A native, who lived at a distance of several days' march, appeared at a mission station and demanded the return of a fruit that he claimed had been stolen from him by someone at the station. Only after thorough questioning did it turn out that he had dreamt the theft and was firmly convinced that a strange person had invaded his personality while he slept. This person was in a position to act in external reality and had obviously robbed him, although nothing was missing from his field.

In our culture, too, groups of associations of this sort arising out of the unconscious have been known since antiquity. The first to describe them in detail was Aristotle in his *Psyche*. There he linked these unconscious part souls with parts of the body and with organs, enumerating a long series of such pairings. In modern medicine, we would say that he had been thinking "psychosomatically." According to von Franz (1992), Chinese folk medicine knows something similar, associating certain complexes with certain bodily centers. Thus there are 365 gods of the body assigned, one by one, to every part of the body, every bodily function, and every inner organ or nerve center.

For all practical purposes, research after Aristotle remained at this level until the last century when the Englishman John Stuart Mill and the German Wilhelm Wundt again took up the problem. Granted, neither spoke of complexes. The term itself is not found in even the largest lexicons until the middle of the nineteenth century, when it was first used in biology. Mill and Wundt studied groups of associations not subject to the conscious will but which nevertheless exercised functions in the psyche. At the end of the century Janet conducted his famous experiments on the dissociation of the personality and the appearance of second personalities in one and the same psyche. In some cases, he was even able to establish the presence of several part personalities, none of whom knew of or had any relationship to the others. However, even if weak, each of these part personalities had a certain degree of consciousness. This later moved Jung to speak of the "conscious luminosity" of the complexes (Jung 1956/63). Janet's case, in which a severely hysterical woman patient was able concurrently to tell her physician the events in her consciousness and, with her left hand, write down what her unconscious complexes were telling her, is very well known.

The first to use the term *complexes* for the unconscious part personalities was Breuer, from whom both Freud and Jung borrowed the concept. Although Freud spoke not a little in his psychoanalysis of complexes—as, for example, the Oedipus complex, the castration complex, the father and mother complexes—these remained for him, as for his followers, of little interest. For Freud, as a natural scientist at the end of nineteenth century, these concepts were too vague, and he followed the original trend of science at the time which was to divide whole phenomena into ever smaller parts, ultimately arriving at the basic constituents, the drives, with which he explained psychic functioning according to the laws of causality.

Through his collaboration with Breuer and the results of his own association experiments, Jung dedicated himself to the intensive exploration of these complex formations in the human psyche; utilizing the association test he had developed, he was almost exclusively concerned with them in the years up until 1909. He even discovered in his own personality one such complex in the form of a "second personality" which he usually called "personality number two" in his writings (Jung 1906-09/73). It might appear that Jung lost interest in complexes after his long and intensive study and a whole series of publications on them. After 1914, he turned more and more to his theory of the archetypes, and in the second half of his life we find the concept of the complex mentioned relatively infrequently in his writings. Nevertheless, in 1934, he was writing that complexes have a certain consciousness and yet he was not certain whether this consciousness belonged as completely to them as it did to the ego-complex.

One must not conclude from Jung's later, extensive occupation with the archetypes and the collective unconscious—a concept which he had to defend against a hostile and unsympathetic scientific community—that he neglected the complexes. His theory of the complexes underwent some alterations in the course of the years. Essentially, in his early writings under Freud's influence, Jung assigned the complexes to the personal unconscious and, to distinguish them, the archetypes to the collective unconscious. Later he modified this in the sense that, indeed, the shell of the complex with its amplifications and associations often resides in the personal unconscious, but the actual core of the complex is native to the collective unconscious. (I discuss this theme in detail in a later chapter.)

An important problem in the theory of the complexes is posed by the fact that even the healthy human psyche is made up of complexes, which means that complexes by no means develop only pathological characteristics but rather are necessary for the healthy development of the psyche and for all new acquisitions in the important phases of the individual's life. The unconscious is, after all, the matrix out of which consciousness first arises, as I discussed in detail in my book on dreams (Dieckmann 1972). In this way, complexes not only can exert a positive effect on the lower, psychosomatic pole of maturation and the development of life extending to the processes of aging but are also capable of developing and solving creative, spiritual, and intellectual processes. A good example of this is the mathematician Poincaré, who von Franz (1992) considers one of the discoverers of the unconscious. She describes episodes in which complexes assisted him in solving difficult problems. Poincaré, looking for an explanation for the so-called automorphous functions, could not find the formula but then saw the solution to the problem in a sort of hypnagogic vision.

In this book, I attempt to fill a lacuna to the extent that I develop a general theory of the complexes which will give both the student and the practicing therapist an overview of this area in terms of diagnosis and therapy. Almost all textbooks of analytical psychology have a chapter on the complexes, but there is no book that presents a differentiated overview of all the possibilities of complex theory. Here I have endeavored to cover the area of diagnosis with the sort of overview that also permits the therapist to grasp an Ariadne thread in the therapy. The latter is especially difficult in the confusing events of a long analysis. In the many individual hours, a long analysis must of course always deal not only with a particular theme but also with a seemingly inextricable tangle of current events, fantasy images, dream contents, and childhood memories as well as associations and amplifications of both subjective and objective nature.

If one attentively observes this tangle from some distance, one discovers that, in most cases, it centers on one or more very specific complexes. This phenomenon caught my attention early on in my analytic work when I discovered how strongly patients were unconsciously identified with the hero or the heroine of their favorite fairy tale (Dieckmann 1967). It is after several decades of activity in the field of C. G. Jung's analytical psychology that I take this further step to develop a more general and more differentiated theory of the complexes that can also be taught to the beginner.

I have included as many clinical examples as possible—case vignettes, as they are usually called—some brief and some that go into greater detail. Of course, these examples have been sufficiently disguised so that the individual cannot be recognized in them.

To facilitate the overview, I use a number of diagrams. I hope that conservative Jungians will forgive me for taking Jung's schema from *Aion* (1959), lifting it out of the more religious domain of the Self and profaning it.

Surely many readers will be struck by the fact that here I mention the extraordinarily important concept of the Self as such. However, those familiar with the material will immediately recognize that, in fact, I am constantly talking about this concept and that it forms the basis of the entire theory. As we know, the archetypal Great Mother and the archetypal Great Father together constitute the Self. If we proceed from the notion, as Jung does, that the healthy psyche is also a complex structure, then it is precisely the concept of this book to deconstruct individual pathological, dominant complexes and replace them with a multitude of complexes that derive from the two great archetypal domains. These overgrown and undeveloped possibilities of the human soul must be laid bare and developed in the course of a careful and often lengthy therapy. This is necessary so that the ego-complex not only has available to it one or two limited possibilities for acting and experiencing in given situations but can enter into relationship with a multitude of complex activities. It is precisely this that would constitute the restoration of the Self and of a healthy functioning of the ego-Self axis.

Conceiving the human psyche as a system of complexes that enters into relationship with another, equally complex, system—namely, that of the physician—in which they mutually affect one another corresponds to modern scientific theories that have long been used in physics and mathematics. Medicine, too, needs new perceptual concepts, as the well-known atomic physicist Capra stated in his book, *The Turning Point* (1982): "our thought, our way of perceiving, and our value concepts must change fundamentally. We need a way of thought that is complex rather than linear, a thought that replaces quantitative measuring with qualitative valuing." This first challenges the physician to observe his own psyche and to create a corresponding balance of complexes in it. Otherwise he is not in a position to treat his patients in terms of complexes. Many years ago we found extensive confirmation of this in our investigations of transference and countertransference (Dieckmann 1971c, 1973; Blomeyer 1971; E. Jung 1973; Wilke 1980). The training analysis that Jung called for early on is intended to achieve this balance in the psyche of the physician. Consequently, it is of uncommon importance. With the exception of individual lucky cases, I would not—in my personal opinion, which surely will irritate many people—think any therapist of any of the too many current "schools" of therapy capable of helping a patient in a differentiated way lest he himself had undergone analysis.

Beyond this, I believe analysis alone does not suffice since, in the transference situation, a good therapist again and again gets into a muddle with his own complex constellations and is forced to clear them up either through the means at his own disposal, for example, by using active imagination, or sometimes with the help of colleagues. In some sense, he has the same plight as the rainmaker of whom the sinologist Richard Wilhelm told this beautiful story:

> Once there was a village where it had not rained for a very long time and there was a dreadful drought. So the villagers decided to put all their money together and to fetch a famous rainmaker from the city. Thereupon the mayor set out, and he succeeded in persuading the rainmaker to come to the village. The first thing he did after he arrived was to spend a whole day walking around all through the village and the fields. Then he ordered the villagers to build him a small, light hut a kilometer outside the town and to leave him there for three days and three nights, only placing a bowl of rice once a day before his door. After these three days, he said, it would rain. And so indeed it happened. He disappeared for three days into his hut, and on the evening of the third day it began to rain. The next day he went to the mayor to collect his reward, which was gladly paid him. But the mayor was curious, and he asked, "Can't you tell me how you did that?" "It was very simple," the rainmaker answered. "When I came from the city to your village, I sensed that something was not in order, and the longer I looked around here, the more disordered I became. So I had you build me a hut and got myself in order again. When I succeeded at that, of course, it began to rain." (Jung 1956/63, p. 419*n*.)

Truly, this is a thought-provoking story which every therapist should take to heart. It also corresponds to what Nietzsche said: "Physician, help thyself, then you will also help your patient" (1965).

On this note I conclude the introduction to this book. Only one thing remains, and that is to express my heartfelt thanks, first of all to my wife, who has supported me in many discussions and ideas as well as transforming the manuscript with the old Latinist's eternally long sentences into a readable German. An equally heartfelt thanks is due my longtime secretary, Fr. Wiegand, for all the corrections and typing, and to the editor at Springer Verlag, who has supported me with word and deed in writing the manuscript.

CHAPTER 1

The Complex Structure of the Psyche

According to the central notion of analytical psychology, complexes are part of the normal phenomena of life; Jung (1948/60a) even said explicitly that they form the structure of the unconscious psyche. Consciousness also has the structure of a complex, and even the ego is to be viewed as a complex formation—with, of course, special tasks and characteristics that distinguish it from other complexes—and because of this, we can view the human psyche as a system that behaves in many respects like an ecological system in nature. The complexes form the individual ecotypes that stand in more or less distinct relationship with one another. Normally, when the system is capable of functioning well, the ego-complex and the Self are responsible for the cohesion and regulation of the system. We must keep in mind, of course, that no human psyche exists by and for itself but always in reference to something else, usually to the people who are close to us or to nature around us. Even the lonely hermit meditating in the wilderness relates his soul to God or, more precisely, to his image of God, which, since it finds expression in his soul, necessarily has a certain anthropomorphic character.

Here, it is not these exceptions but rather what is commonplace, what we usually encounter in our life and in our practice, that we want to study first. In comprehending and describing the structure of the human psyche in terms of complexes, we immediately encounter a difficulty that has to do with their multitude and indefiniteness. If we survey the analytic literature, not only in analytical psychology but also in psychoanalysis, we find many different human characteristics and forms of experience to which the concept of the complex is attached. For example, there is a group of general complexes that rest on characteristics, attitudes, or behaviors such as inferiority and superiority complexes, or, deriving from the latter, a genius complex; there is a victim complex, an intimacy complex, a whole list of complexes of this sort that could be extended *ad infinitum*.

Another group of complexes are those that can be derived from the demands of the human drives, for instance, a sex complex, a recognition complex, a power complex, a greed complex, or an envy complex. This list, too, can be augmented according to the number of human drives that various authors currently assume exist.

Finally, in the literature of analytical psychology, there is yet a third group of complexes based on the notion of archetypal images. Since the complex in analytical psychology is always seen forming around an archetypal core—as Jacobi (1959) described in detail and to which theme we will return when we discuss the formation and structure of the complex—the number of possible complexes again corresponds to the number of inherent archetypes in the human psyche. Although not infinite, this number, as we see from the colorful array of mythological figures, is incredibly high and the possibilities actually impossible to list. Two complexes arising from this domain—the first to be described and certainly the most important to date—are the Oedipus complex, first elaborated by Freud in his *Interpretation of Dreams*, and the Jonah-and-the-whale complex, which decisively rules the preoedipal period and is described by Jung in *The Psychology of the Unconscious* (usually known as *Symbols of Transformation*, 1912/56). Subsequently a great number of archetypal complexes have been described. I will cite only a few examples that have been presented in the literature of analytical psychology in recent years. There is a book by Perera (1986) on the scapegoat complex; Wilke (1977) describes an authority complex, Rentrop (1978) a messiah complex, von Raffay (1981) the Solomon complex, Bach (1972) "his father's son" complex, and finally, Aigrisse (1964) a Don Juan complex. These are only a few, which I found where the figure of the complex forms part of the title of a book or study. I have ignored the many authors who mention certain complexes in their writings, as these are intended only as examples which one can augment at will corresponding to the images of mythology, ethnology, religion, history, literature, and so on.

An additional category of complexes of the psyche is that of the stations of the individuation process. Here we have a quite manageable number of complexes, such as the persona, the shadow, the animus or anima, and the self complexes. This division is used by a number of analytical psychologists, both practically and clinically. Without a doubt, one of these complex areas stands in the foreground for each patient, especially at the beginning of treatment, and the therapy often circles about it for a long time.

Finally, we can consider complexes in terms of a person's significant relationships, such as Bach in the above-mentioned his-father's-son complex, or as Jung (1954/59) did in the case of the mother complex of the daughter. Here we have first a mother complex and a father complex, to which we can add the sibling complexes according to gender and position in the family, the grandparent complexes, and then complexes around the more distant members of the family, such as uncles and aunts, with whom the patient may identify to a greater or lesser degree such that this identification acquires the character of a complex. It happens not at all infrequently, when the father or mother is difficult to accept, that one reaches out to other persons in the family clan with identifications and idealizations. This can go far back in the ancestral line, as illustrated in the following example.

Not so long ago I conducted the control analysis of a patient who had a very weak and unsuccessful father. In contrast, his mother's family held a string of colorful and quite successful men. Among them was a famous robber chieftain distantly related from centuries past, the so-called *Schinderhannes*, Johnny the Butcher, who did his mischief in the forests of Hunsrück. The literature, and also the film made about him, styled him as a sort of Robin Hood figure, a robber who, with his large and powerful band, plundered the rich and gave to the poor, having been forced upon this path by an outrageous injustice. Ultimately, he was set upon by a large contingent of military, surrounded, and seized after an intense battle. In the end, he was condemned along with his accomplices and hanged. From early childhood, the patient's psyche was fascinated by this figure, and he unconsciously identified with him in many respects. Characteristic of this were his unconventional protest stance against rigid norms he could not accept, a distinct level of courage, and a corresponding slyness and cleverness in discovering unknown ways and possibilities for moving about in a kind of gray area. But his life, like all his undertakings, was inhibited, blocked by a deep-seated anxiety that accompanied his actions always; in the background lurked the nasty end of *Schinderhannes* in chains at the end of the hangman's rope. Of course, this was fully unconscious; his anxiety began to abate only as consciousness gradually dawned and his identification with this figure as a surrogate father began to loosen.

This sort of Johnny the Butcher belongs to the shadow side of the father archetype while other "lighter" heroes from myth, fairy tale, or personal lineage with which patients identify belong to the bright upper realm of the archetype.

Hence, in my judgment, all the other complexes can be derived from these two great fundamental complexes, the mother complex and the father complex. This includes the brother and sister complexes in so far as brother or sister are more or less a rejuvenated edition of father or mother. We know from all analyses the extent to which the parental complexes play into the rivalries among siblings. In her classic book, *Analysis of Children* (1930), Wickes elaborated for the first time the extent to which children live, suffer, and express the unconscious problems and complexes of their parents.

It is not difficult to derive all the other complexes from the two parental complexes. I would like to illustrate this with an example. Among others, the archetype of the hero, whether a positive or a negative hero, belongs among the core elements of the father complex (which I will discuss at length and in detail later). From the viewpoint of mythology, all the various hero figures—those with which the ego can identify and that Campbell (1949) has described in *Hero with a Thousand Faces*—find their place in a hero complex. When this sort of identification takes place, a superiority or inferiority complex can arise simultaneously. Alternatively, the hero archetype may enter into the ego ideal or the superego and from that position exert excessive pressure for accomplishment on the ego, which can then lead to an inferiority complex.

If the hero is a Don Juan or a Casanova, erotic or sexual complexes can in turn arise from this root. Negative hero images—such as the robber chieftain mentioned earlier—can trigger anxiety complexes. If a successful hero is projected onto the brother as a rejuvenated father, sibling rivalries and complexes arise, again accompanied by corresponding inferiority or superiority complexes, which then can fall within the domain of a power complex.

In the case of a woman, the archetype of the paternal hero can form the animus or a part of the animus. Depending on the identification, it can then lead, in the healthy sense, to courageous and uncommon opinions, views, and behaviors, or, in a pathological identification, to an excessively aggressive or completely unadapted stance. If an animus of this sort is projected onto the men around her, they will most likely be overwhelmed and unable to fulfill the wishes and expectations of the woman.

We could enlarge this list considerably with the ramifications proceeding from this sort of core element of a complex and continuing give rise to additional complexes that actually belong to the original complex. The examples mentioned here are intended to give only a glimpse into the abundance of possible derivative forms. Of course, I do not mean that general complexes—as, for example, the inferiority, power, sexual, or aggression complexes—can be derived solely from the one specific core element of the father complex. It goes without saying that they can arise from the core of either the father complex or the mother complex, for example, from the senex archetype, from a mother deity, from a witch, and from many others.

Precisely for this reason—that is, because of the abundance of possibilities for derivation—it is diagnostically as well as clinically appropriate to give precedence to the latter classification of the complexes. A diagnostic that referred only to each of the various archetypes must necessarily burst all bounds as it compiles ever more and varied complexes. While these have the advantage of granting limitless room for the creativity of the individual, such abundance creates difficulties for the beginner by which he or she comes to grief. Likewise, this method would lead to chaos about which we could do nothing in terms of the possibility of scientific comparison;

and of course the possibility of comparison is something upon which we are absolutely dependent.

A further difficulty would arise if we were to classify, diagnose, and treat the complexes according to the stations on the path of individuation, that is, according to persona, shadow, anima, animus, or self. For a period of time, I attempted to do this in my clinical notes, but I came to grief again and again on certain classifications and difficulties. Where, for example, should one situate a mother complex in this scheme? Does it belong to the Self even though it is only a part of the Self, since the Self is formed in concert by the archetypes of the Great Father and the Great Mother? Or should we situate it in the anima, at least in the case of a man, and in the shadow for a woman? Granted, both the man's anima and the woman's shadow are formed out of the maternal realm, but do they still belong there? I think not. Even if the anima has elements of the personal mother, she (the anima) will have incorporated other elements. It does not seem correct to equate an anima complex with the mother, and it becomes too circumstantial to explain in detail what other elements are also present each time. This holds true not only for this example; a multitude of other complexes are just as difficult to house in this schema.

We would, of course, make it far too easy for ourselves if we reduced the entire psychodynamics of the human soul to two simple complexes, such as the mother and the father complexes. It is necessary to differentiate them. The first step in differentiation was taken by Jung himself when he distinguished between a positive and a negative mother complex in his essay, "Psychological Aspects of the Mother Archetype" (1954/68). (In other passages, Jung usually writes only of a mother or a father complex.) In this essay, he identifies the positive mother complex with a far-reaching identity with the mother (or with the archetypal maternal), whereas the negative mother complex consists of an extensive rejection of and alienation from the same elements. We can easily apply this to the father complex so that we now can speak of four different categories of these complexes. Thus, in the patient, we can diagnose a negative or positive mother complex or a negative or positive father complex.

A diagnosis of this sort—which, by the way, also plays a considerable role with the patient in the therapeutic handling of analytic treatment, as I will elaborate later in detail—comes not only from the unconscious but draws in the attitude of the conscious ego-complex to a large extent. With many patients, it can be established with relative ease in the first few sessions. The negative complex is revealed by a more or less clear rejection of the parental figure and contains predominantly aggressive libido. A typical conscious statement of this would be: "There is no way I want to be like my mother (or my father)." On the other hand, the patient's statements about the parental figure may at first sound thoroughly positive or neutral, yet the critical observer may clearly detect a devaluative or negative accent slipped in by the unconscious. Such subtlety makes diagnosis more difficult, particularly for the beginner. Here it becomes less a question of the formulation of the associations than of the emotional undertone and associations. I am reminded of a famous quote from Shakespeare: "But Caesar is an honorable man." The same holds true for the positive parental complex, where many expressions may sound critical or negative, yet below the surface one clearly hears the idealization. In chapter 8 on the positive mother archetype I cite Chagall's statement about his mother, which had such an ominous effect nobody dared speak to her. But at the end of this passage in his autobiography, she turns back into a queen through his idealization of her. This is not always expressed so clearly, but one can often hear it echoing in the background.

In *The Great Mother* (1955), Neumann made a further differentiation that is applicable in many cases and valuable not only in regard to the mother complex but also to the father complex. The distinction has to do with differentiating an "elementary character" from a "transformative character." Neumann illustrates this with many archetypal-mythological examples (see Neumann's diagram of the various aspects of the Great Mother). Neumann distinguishes positive and negative elementary and transformative characters. Under the positive elementary character are subsumed characteristics such as giving birth, liberating, constructing, being born again, rebirth. The negative aspect, in contrast, subsumes holding fast, capturing, diminishing, illness, and death. On the other side are the characteristics of the positive transformative character: giving, increasing, inspiration, ecstasy, vision, and wisdom; the negative qualities are rejection, withdrawal, dissolution, madness, addiction, and benumbing. In the background of the personal parental complexes these two characters often can be differentiated precisely because the archetypal always shines through the personal and gives the latter its particular accent. Naturally, it is always only an accent: seldom do we encounter a pure elementary or transformative character since here, as everywhere in human life, the extremes are extraordinarily infrequent. However, in my opinion, these components offer a certain prognostic hint. An extremely rigid (elementary) parental component that forms the dominant complex confronts therapy with considerably greater resistance. The superego elements permit no change or transformation of the rigid, often moralizing patterns of experience and behavior; they punish deviations with severe guilt feelings. If at least some transformative elements are contained in the complex, it is often easier to loosen and transform it.

To review what we have said so far, the two original complexes—father and mother—have now given rise to eight different diagnostic categories:

A. Mother complex

    1) positive

    2) negative

    3) elementary character

    4) transformative character

B. Father complex

    1) positive

    2) negative

    3) elementary character

    4) transformative character

As mentioned earlier, these categories are not only of diagnostic significance, but often of considerable therapeutic significance. As subsequent examples will show, positive as well as negative complexes with their idealizations and demonizations reach back even into the collective unconscious. Nevertheless, the therapeutic stance is to pay careful attention to not allowing a negative mother figure as a complex to persist in the analysis, but rather to mobilizing the opposite pole at the right time, which of course applies equally to the positive mother complex. In my experience, especially in many control analyses and from much literature pointing in this direction, there is a tendency to ascribe the child's neuroses to the parents' failure to socialize the child and then, until the end of the analysis, to regard the parents as negative parental imagos whose detrimental introject will be replaced by the introjection of the positive analyst father or analyst mother. But the complex is preserved, not dissolved, with all the attendant dangers of relapse. There are no entirely evil parents, even among those that suffer the most severe psychic illnesses. Every human being is a mixture of good and evil, white and black, positive and negative. It is only the archetypes that are strictly one-sided, for which reason they are called *types*, not people. Every good and successful analysis therefore has the task of mobilizing the opposite pole and allowing the human being within to be seen behind the projected complex in all of his or her ambivalence. Where this is no longer possible, for example, due to the early death of the parent who carries the idealized or demonized projection, the counter pole, as the complement, must be worked out with people in the intimate environment or in the archetypal realm.

Moreover, the process of socialization is incomparably more complex than what can be reduced to the introjection of the figures of the personal parents. We still know very little about the genetic components that play a role in the development of the human psyche and neuroses. We know only that their influence is certainly greater than earlier analysts, who, not entirely without justification, went to the opposite extreme following the teaching of the genetically fixed character in the nineteenth century, wanted to admit. Contemporary twin research, for example, that of Schepank (1975) on stuttering, reveals a definite genetic component. If we read the work on infant observation carefully, especially Mahler (1975), we are struck by how various children can react independent of their mothers.

In his conception of the archetype per se—that is, the inheritance of a pure structure that the cultural environment fills out with the corresponding cultural imagery, in part consciously, in part unconsciously—Jung pointed out what great influence the culture surrounding us exerts on the collective unconscious and thereby on the development of our psyche. Fromm (1936) took up this idea, conceptualizing fathers and mothers, along with his corresponding ideas and concepts, more as prototypes of the social field. Werblowsky (1987) advanced the theory that an unconscious identification with the culture of the surrounding environment takes place that can be observed, for example, in the linguistic behavior of Chinese children who as infants were placed in Japanese families (and of Japanese children placed in Chinese families) and who later were no longer able to learn, let alone pronounce, certain sounds in their native tongue. Thus Japanese children who grew up with Chinese mothers in China cannot pronounce the "r" sound, which previously was regarded as a genetically determined trait for the Chinese. From all these examples, we can gauge what an essential role is played by the various levels of the collective unconscious. According to one notion in analytical psychology, the projection of all these collective elements lies on the personal parents. They also form the essential elements of the parental complexes, and only gradually in the course of individuation are they withdrawn.

Having clarified that the various functional divisions of the complexes can all find a place in the parental complexes, I suggest this classification be considered fundamental. In both practice and theory, as outlined by Jung, the individuation process, with its various stages and complex formations, is always an interplay among the personal and archetypal parental imagos, ego development, and the collective consciousness, in which the latter, including superego formation, arises out of the spiritual side of the parental archetypes (Jacobi 1967). The Self consists of the combination of the Great Mother and the Great Father. Anima and animus, as well as shadow and persona, have their origins there, elements of which are preserved to a considerable extent even in an advanced individuation far along the course of life.

An example of shadow formation will clarify this. The mother of a thirty-two-year-old woman patient moved with her husband and four children, of whom my patient was the oldest, to a metropolis from the village in which they lived. The patient was fourteen at the time. Her mother worked temporarily as a prostitute in the city, which caused a great scandal in the village when it became known. Thereupon the father decided to move to another town, where he married again. On the basis of a negative mother complex and a total rejection of her prostitute mother, this patient erected a powerful defense against unrelated sexuality. Sexuality, so she idealized, was permissible only in a relationship of pure personal love for another, and one must never let oneself fall so low that one forgot this personal feeling. To her great distress, and accompanied by considerable inferiority feelings, the patient was never able to achieve orgasm in her relationships, and only after lengthy analysis was she able to admit this. In her dreams, however, prostitutes, brothels, bars, and nightlife in every form regularly turned up, at first defensively projected onto other women and associated with feelings of disgust. Not until the patient was able to experience herself in a dream in a brothel as a prostitute having lusty sex with an unknown man could she begin to integrate the necessary aspect of transpersonal sexuality and the task of I and Thou in orgasm. In this case, it is important to note that, unlike her mother, she did not act out her prostitute shadow but rather was able to include a part of the transpersonal experience of the negative Great Mother as the Great Whore in her personal relationship. It was precisely that part that had hindered her own capacity for orgasm as long as it was an unconscious shadow quality and that had caused her such severe inferiority feelings.

In closing, let us repeat that Jung assumes a complex structure for the entire psyche. This includes both consciousness and the unconscious, and even the ego has the structure of a complex. This corresponds to his theory of the quantitatively, but *not* qualitatively fixed libido, whose energetic potential arises via the tension of opposites between two complexes (Jung 1948/60b). Here Jung takes a phylogenetic standpoint according to which every healthy aspect of the soul forms a complex. Neuroses arise when consciousness assumes a wrong attitude toward the unconscious that may be evoked not only by ego defects or faulty ego development but equally by the excessively strong energy of unconscious complexes, something I will discuss in greater detail in the chapter on borderline phenomena.

Hence complexes belong to the fundamental structure of the psyche and place us human beings in conflicts which it is our task to suffer and to resolve. In Jung's view, suffering in human life is never an illness as such; rather, it presents the opposite pole to happiness, and the one is unthinkable without the other. A complex becomes pathogenic only when it is repressed, suppressed, or denied in that we think that we don't have it. A complex turns into a negative and disruptive element in the psyche only due to the ego-complex's insufficient capacity to face it. Having it out and coming to terms with complexes serves the individuation process and accordingly is to be viewed as something positive.

There are complexes that have never entered consciousness and that therefore have never been repressed. These complexes arise primarily from the collective unconscious. The unconscious is, of course, the matrix out of which consciousness arises in the first place. Thus the collective unconscious represents an autonomous functional complex with an inherent, primary structure in which, as in a seed, the typical developmental and maturational possibilities of the human psyche are latent. The collective unconscious has a prospective character since, by creating the images in the cores of the complexes, it is in the position of linking them with drive energies and imparting meaning and direction to them. I have elaborated this at greater length in my work on dream interpretation (Dieckmann 1972).

CHAPTER 2

The Structure of Complexes

If we wish to inquire into the structure of a complex, we must first ask what we actually understand by the term *complex*. By means of his experimental researches, recorded in a group of essays collectively titled "Studies in Word Association" (1906-09/73), Jung discovered the emotionally toned complexes. In his word association experiments he found that certain stimulus words that were more emotionally charged for the test subject altered the subject's typical response behavior. Specifically, the altered responses appeared in reaction times, misunderstandings and repetitions of the stimulus word, lack of reaction, or slips of the tongue. Since these "mistakes" occurred again and again when the test was repeated with the same stimulus words, Jung inferred that some inner disturbance was at work. The inner disturbance was elicited by a group of related, emotion-laden elements that he called "complexes."

At first, Jung thought that these elements were always negatively toned. But as early as 1915, Hoffmann demonstrated in his dissertation that pleasurable elements could interfere with the course of the experiment, although they did not interfere as strongly as the negative ones. Hence it was established that not only negative emotionally toned complexes, but also positive ones, could exert a disruptive effect on consciousness and thus be subject to defenses.

A complex, therefore, behaves in a certain sense like a split-off part of the psyche, comparable to the notion of part-egos that result from tensions and conflicts among conscious and unconscious tensions within the whole ego, a notion put forth by recent British psychoanalysts. Fairbairn, Winnicott, Guntrip, and Sutherland in particular are associated with this concept. The British psychoanalysts, however, proceed only from the ego-complex while Jung's concept also takes into account those complexes that arise from the collective unconscious as new psychic acquisitions that contain no ego components. For these, Jung spoke only of "luminosities" (Jung 1956/63), as he called them in *Mysterium Coniunctionis*. Otherwise, these part-egos of the British school, as psychic subsystems or split-off ecotypes (as modern ecology would call them), correspond fully to Jung's concept of the complex, and it is rather astonishing how, even today, these authors desperately avoid any mention of Jung.

Early on, Jung recognized the systematic character of psychic processes, and already in his 1934 lecture, "A Review of the Complex Theory" (1948/60a), he demonstrated that there were no isolated psychic processes. In the same essay, he introduced the idea that complexes become constellated, in which "the outward situation releases a psychic process in which certain contents gather together and prepare for action" (par. 198, p. 94) Constellating is an automatic process that cannot be hindered since complexes possess their own psychic energy. Jung compared this constellating psychic contents with the function of a magnet that collects iron filings in a specific form. This image is, of course, two-dimensional whereas the content of complexes are to be thought of as three-dimensional structures, if not four-dimensional since there is also a time component that often does not coincide with the time frame of the conscious parts of the ego-complex. It is usually the case that the constellated complex is younger than the ego-complex, deriving from earlier times and capturing in its structure earlier ways of experiencing and behaving. At times, however, it can speak like an older, more mature personality, but this is quickly forgotten, not taken up as an ongoing attitude. This group also includes the complexes that elicit synchronistic phenomena such as von Franz describes in her book, *Psyche and Matter* (1922).

A simple example from the analysis of a thirty-two-year-old woman patient illustrates how she regressed to a distinctly younger psychic condition in certain situations.

One of her problems was that, after a period of happiness in her relationship with a man, she ran into violent difficulties with him. She felt he no longer understood her, that he chauvinistically exploited her and rejected her. It reached the point where she broke off the relationship or the man withdrew. Finally she began a relationship with a much younger man, an Italian high school senior whom she had gotten to know while working evenings as an assistant tutor. Naturally, I had an inner reaction of some concern and skepticism toward this liaison, especially since I could see from her accounts that the young man had great difficulties with this relationship and was reacting to her with obviously strong ambivalence. Up until this point in the analysis, I had been a permissive and consistently benevolent father figure for her. But because of my inner attitude and the tenor of certain interpretations, the situation changed rather abruptly. The complex was constellated between us almost imperceptibly at first; I became (in her eyes) a chauvinistic man who no longer understood her and with whom she could no longer work on her problem with the young man, about which she had said nothing at first. At the same time, her voice became squeaky and less distinct, and she began to cast her glance down often; in some hours, she turned more and more into something resembling a rather aged and tortured teenager. Many aspects of her *puer aeternus* infatuation could be analyzed and brought to consciousness, but that did nothing to alter the situation. The resolution of the complex came only when she finally brought the problem into the transference and explained to me that she felt I no longer accepted and understood her. At the same time, she was able to express to me feelings of intense anger and pain which had gone so far that she had fantasies of terminating the analysis. At first, neither of us quite knew what was happening. Only gradually was I able, by using differentiated questioning, to link her feelings to concrete situations and expressions involving me.

The background that finally came to light was this: she projected onto me a stern father who forbid all sexuality and who reacted with ill-humor and rejection to every young man who approached her. Correspondingly, in spite of all better, more rational insight, she understood each of my interpretations in this way, that is, as devaluative, judgmental, and disapproving. Nor was she able to ask what my comments meant, since in this respect her father had been completely unapproachable. Only when she gradually learned to do this, and as all her deep fears about men and sexuality still present in the background came out, was she able to withdraw the projections and her complex dissolved. Simultaneously, she regained an age-appropriate personality and gradually learned to be more inquisitive in her relationships and to interact more understandingly with other people.

Let us describe what Jung understands with the term *complex* and how he defines it. He writes:

What then, scientifically speaking, is a "feeling-toned complex"? It is the *image* of a certain psychic situation which is strongly accentuated emotionally and is, moreover, incompatible with the habitual attitude of consciousness. This image has a powerful inner coherence, it has its own wholeness and, in addition, a relatively high degree of autonomy, so that it is subject to the control of the conscious mind to only a limited extent, and therefore behaves like an animated foreign body in the sphere of consciousness. The complex can usually be suppressed with an effort of will, but not argued out of existence, and at the first suitable opportunity it reappears in all its original strength. (Jung, 1948/60a, p. 96)

Further, Jung refers to the research work of Janet and Prince who succeeded in demonstrating fourfold and fivefold splitting of the personality. In these splits, each part personality had its own character and memory to which consciousness had no access or only a limited degree of access.

Grof (1983) has demonstrated in his research work with persons under the influence of LSD the same results in which individual part personalities could be traced back into early childhood and, in some cases, back through the ancestral line. I was able to observe this sort of complex, corresponding to a "double personality," in the analysis of a patient who suffered pathological states of intoxication in which he had a completely different personality (Dieckmann 1978a). In his early dissertation, Jung (1902/70) described a case in which a complex of this sort formed an unconscious part personality with a different character, although at that time he did not use the term *complex*, which later was to play such a great role in his psychology.

The great poets have been aware of these part personalities with the character of a complex and have described them as figures in their works. Perhaps most well known is Goethe's Faust with two souls dwelling in his breast. We also find this sort of process very clearly in Tolstoy's novel, *Resurrection* (1913). Here Maslova, the main female character, is forced to repress her entire earlier personality as a happy, affectionate, and selfless girl when she must enter the milieu of the prostitute. Tolstoy powerfully describes this repression as she attempts, with all her strength, and successfully, to extinguish from her memory the woman she used to be in order to become a calculating, coquettish harlot exploiting men. Nevertheless, the old personality is preserved in her; it shines through again and again and ultimately reenters consciousness and becomes dominant in a more mature form through her sacrifice and relationship with her first seducer, Prince Nechludov. The poet describes the same phenomenon in Nechludov, who was probably to a great extent an autobiographical figure for Tolstoy. He also depicted here the unrelenting conflict between an egocentric person, indifferent to the sufferings of others, and a helpful, idealistic person full of compassion and relatedness.

Analytical psychology always proceeds from the assumption of health and views pathology as a one-sided overemphasis of a certain aspect of the psyche; hence in analytical psychology we conceive complexes as part of the normal life of the psyche. We even regard them and their specific energy as the basis of all psychic functioning. In analogy to nature, we can call complexes "force fields" or "maps" of the psyche, to use an expression of Seifert's (1981). In the macrocosm of our earth, we encounter the most varied landscapes: meadows, forests, deserts, swamps, oceans, rivers. All are interlinked in some way, and the well-being of the whole is assured only if no one of them gains the upper hand and overwhelms everything else. We may view the complexes analogously. In the healthy psyche, an entire system of different complexes, each with its unique quality, are related to one another. Through a partial identification, the healthy ego can make use of them when necessitated by various life situations to master the task at hand.

A complex turns pathological in one of only two ways. First it can draw excessive energy to itself, which we can understand from our (personal) developmental history, because it contains very early, deep feelings of love or hate also linked with equally deep fears and aggressive impulses. Second, it can become pathological if split off and isolated from the rest of the psyche as a consequence of these overpowering energies and the excessive accumulation of associations and amplifications they bring about. Then, like a dictator who arrogates all power to himself, the complex tends to suppress and repress everything that will not fit in its frame of reference, and this causes the conscious ego-complex to act again and again in self-damaging and overtaxing ways that would be avoided if it could reflect rationally. I am reminded of a relatively young patient who obviously had a hero complex that, like Hercules, again and again made him take on unfulfillable tasks. In trying to master them, he completely overtaxed himself, forgot or neglected everything else in his life, including his family, and would end up dead tired. But if he did succeed in accomplishing a given task, he was never proud and satisfied; rather, he sank into deep depression or, like the ancient Hercules, experienced wild outbreaks of aggression directed against himself.

Let us take another look at what we have already discussed in general terms, but now focusing on the elements out of which the complex is actually formed. First we have what is called the shell of the complex. It consists of all the associations and amplifications that collect around the complex, continually enriched in the course of life. On the one hand, these associations and amplifications consist of actual experiences and of the subjective experience of certain realities, a process that is ongoing in us to the extent that objective and subjective experiences actually or apparently conform to the meaning of the complex. On the other hand, all the fantasies that we creatively develop or take in from other people, literature, shared traditions, artistic expressions, or other sources, contribute to shell of the complex. Here we can also observe that contents seemingly unrelated to the complex can be drawn in and distorted to fit the complex, especially when the complex has become pathological and carries a high energy charge. Thus, as we will later see in a clinical example, a neutral person's friendly smile can be experienced as ridicule and deeply felt wounding in the case of a paranoid complex. Expressed in a simple, two-dimensional graphic, the complex would appear as represented in figure 2.1.

The black dot in the middle represents the core of the complex while the

FIGURE 2.1 The complex, enriched with associations
Jacobi (1962) with modifications by the author

straight and curved lines represent the partly subjective, partly objective associations the core has attracted. (The curved lines represent certain contents that the complex "bends" or distorts so that they no longer correspond to their original meaning or to consensual reality.)

Complexes are interlinked, particularly in the healthy psyche, and a single complex never exists solitarily, which we can also represent in a diagram. We must, of course, keep in mind that these sorts of diagrams can only be visual aids. Like everything having to do with the psyche, the actual structure of a complex cannot be made visible. The psyche is obviously a multidimensional structure that we can understand only from its effects. All our experience leads us to infer that complexes, even in their greatly varied forms, are interlinked, either directly or indirectly.

When complexes are directly interlinked, each individual complex is connected to another complex via specific associations that touch the two (or more) complexes. When complexes are indirectly interlinked, the first complex is linked with the second, the second with a third, the third with a fourth, etc. Hence we would speak of a direct interlinking if a woman's animus complex showed a correspondence with certain attitudes and behaviors of her father complex. On the other hand, the interlinking would be indirect if the animus complex was completely unlike the personal father. Such a complex might correspond, for example, to the idealized image of the maternal grandfather, who for his part, corresponded to certain shadow aspects of her father (aspects that the woman repressed or did not even perceive). In this case, the woman would have related unconsciously to her father's shadow when making her choice of partner.

In representing a direct interlinking in which each complex connects with every other complex directly, the simplest model is that of the transference quaternio (figure 2.2).

FIGURE 2.2

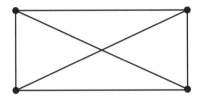

Here the four complexes are represented by four black dots that are connected to one another by lines. Each of the four complexes is directly interlinked with the other three without the intermediary of another complex. By contrast, an "indirect" interlinking could be represented as in figure 2.3.

FIGURE 2.3

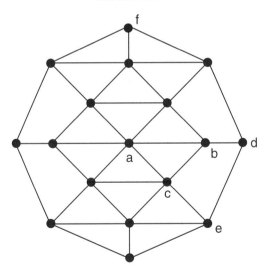

This diagram clearly illustrates that complex *a*, situated in the middle, can come into association with complexes *d* or *e* only via complex *b* or complex *c* wherein a common or adequately similar association mobilizes first the one and then the next complex. It is still more difficult for complex *a* to reach complex *f*, since in order to do so, at least two intermediate complexes would have to be activated. If *a* is relatively close to consciousness and consciousness is able to experience it, then complex *f* is quite distant from consciousness, and we might assume that consciousness is unlikely to gain any knowledge of the existence of this distant complex.

Some complexes remain unconscious because the development of personality has not yet required or permitted them to enter consciousness. Other "distant" and dissociated complexes have arisen in the course of the individual's personal development as described above. In our daily work with patients, we usually encounter first the dark, negative aspects of the great parental imagoes. For a long time we have to work very hard to bring to consciousness the deep feelings of disappointment, hate, devaluation, destructive aggression, envy, inferiority, and so on. These feelings are incompatible with the moral personality and with the demands of the superego, and for both parties, the analyst and the analysand, they are difficult to tolerate in the countertransference. All the deprivation, lack of understanding, parental arbitrariness, egotism, inadequate empathy, and lack of emotionality that was experienced in early childhood as a deep wounding must first be worked through. And while working through all this, one must not forget that not only the negative parental complexes may be partially or extensively unconscious, but the positive aspects may have been repressed, too. Linda Leonard (1982) offers a beautiful example from her own experience. She describes a father complex, consciously experienced as negative. Her father was alcoholic; to a large degree, she and her family devalued him and experienced him as destructive. Only after a long analysis was she able to see the positive Dionysian side of her father and realize this potential in herself. I referred to this phenomenon earlier in reference to Tolstoy's *Resurrection*, where the two main characters repress positive values, as a complex, in a part personality.

In conclusion, I would like to call to the reader's attention the observation that complexes are not limited only to individuals but can seize hold of entire groups. Seifert (1981) remarks that the complex of national greatness or of the master race can call forth changes that move the world. Even when complexes are not pathological, they belong, as Jung has discussed (1948/60a), to the most characteristic phenomena in the psyche, both in differentiated and in more primitive groups or peoples. In this context, he mentions some examples from ancient literature: the Gilgamesh epic depicts a power complex, and the Book of Tobias in the Bible offers the example of an erotic complex and its cure. We have studied these sorts of collective complexes very thoroughly in a working group at the Berlin Jung Institute and edited the studies (Dieckmann and Springer 1988), so I will not elaborate on this theme here.

CHAPTER 3

The Relationships of the Ego-complex to the Individual Complexes

Before I present two rather detailed examples of the development and structure of the shell and the core of a complex, as I have conceptualized them from my clinical experience, I would like to describe the effects and relationships that the ego-complex may have on and with the various complexes. Since the psychology, and especially the pathology, of the ego and its disturbances and defenses has been thoroughly researched and described by the Freudian school over the last decades, we can forego discussing this here. Surely it does not make sense for us in analytical psychology to create our own terminology for something for which there is already a vocabulary that names phenomena identical to what we have observed empirically and worked with clinically. Of course, it would make sense for an analyst of our school to work out a generally accepted schema of ego development and the attendant disturbances that can occur, perhaps following Erich Neumann's (1963/73) concepts or Kadinsky's (1964) ideas about types. This would be a valuable supplement to the knowledge that we now have about the ego and its defenses, or it might be an independent working hypothesis that would serve us better than what we now have.

In my description of the various forms in which complexes affect the ego-complex, I will rely to a great extent on Jacobi's (1959) and Whitmont's (1969) elaborations. I am also adopting Whitmont's differentiation of identification (as a process closer to consciousness) and identity (as a completely unconscious process).

It is a good idea to remember that, as a rule, complexes are characterized by three features: they tend 1) to be uncorrectable; 2) to operate automatically; and 3) to enrich themselves with archaic, mythological amplifications.

This means that even the purely rational knowledge that one has a complex does not put one in a position to resolve, modify, or work through it. Not only do we have complexes, but they have us, and at most we can suppress or repress them. Every complex commands a relatively high degree of autonomy and is subject to will and conscious desires only to a limited degree. Here again we have the part personalities within the psyche already mentioned, which usually behave completely willfully. The further removed from consciousness a complex becomes and the stronger the energy it contains, the more it tends to include mythological and archaic images from the collective unconscious in its repertory of active imagery.

As is true about the description of all organic objects, so too in the case of the complex we must take into account the historical dimension in order to grasp the dynamic process. The three types of time always participate in the origin of a complex: past, present, and future. The first corresponds to the infantile roots, that is, the influences of the inner and outer worlds of childhood and of the history of the individual's life with all its subjective experiences. The present of the complex corresponds to the actual, current conflict in which the individual is embroiled. The future corresponds to the "finalistic" component. Every complex, as well as every symbol, contains a trend, a movement toward some end point or condition or resolution. Again and again, Jung emphasized the finalistic point of view in contrast to Freud's purely causal analysis. With all this in mind, we can now discuss the various ways the complex can exert its effects on the ego-complex.

1) The complex may be unconscious but not very strongly charged. In this case, it blocks the normal flow of psychic events only at a few junctures and finds expression in small errors in behavior or in minor symptoms that the person concerned does not view as pathological. Typical examples are the subject of Freud's famous book, *The Psychopathology of Everyday Life*, in which he presents a multitude of these sorts of "errors" or "mistakes," such as saying the wrong thing, forgetting, misreading, writing errors, and so on. For example, a complex consisting of a somewhat intensified, latent homosexuality that carries a certain difficulty in relationships to persons of the same sex with either too much or too little distance or an increased frequency of conflict might come under this heading. The complex, as such, is relatively well integrated into the totality of the psyche and causes no seriously pathological symptoms. Here we reach the shifting boundary between health and sickness that no physician has ever been able to determine precisely.

2) The complex may be such that its affective energy is greatly elevated and enriched so that it positions itself in opposition to the conscious ego, as a sort of "second" ego. This threatens to tear the individual in two insofar as he or she is drawn back and forth between two contradictory groups of

images. A well-known mythological image of this situation is the Sinis Pityocamptes, from the Theseus saga, who waylaid travelers, bound them between two bent pine trees, and then released the trees, tearing the hapless travelers apart. Theseus overpowered him and freed the Pelepones from this robber. We frequently find a pathological example of this in certain cases of compulsion neurosis in which the patient's inability to chose is marked.

> Many years ago, before the Berlin Wall was erected, I had a student in treatment with me who, for weeks and weeks, spent many hours considering whether he should buy his textbooks in the East or the West. In East Berlin they were considerably less expensive, but he had scruples about depriving the poorer people there. On the other hand, penalizing the godless in the East corresponded to his more Christian-colored ideology. Purchasing his books in the West, however, demanded a considerable sacrifice for him, and all his classmates of course bought in the East. But on the other hand, he condemned the greedy capitalism in the West and did not realize that he was supporting it by paying the high prices that were demanded of poor students.

3) An even stronger form is marked by the appearance of a "double personality." Here the complex is completely freed from the psychic context and appears as a part personality in its own right. (I offered examples of this above, p. 14, in the case of the patient with pathological states of intoxication and in the well-known literary treatment of this theme in Stevenson's *Dr. Jekyll and Mr. Hyde.*)

4) At the fourth level, the ego identifies partially or even completely with the complex. We recognize this condition, at least as a transient phenomenon with self-healing tendencies, in people who are "in love," when a man or a woman is completely possessed by his or her partner or by the corresponding inner image, that is, the anima or animus. Partial identification is accompanied by disturbances in adaptation, a relative loss of a sense of reality, as well as some degree of emotional vulnerability. In the case of a complete identification or of an identity of the ego and the complex, a condition of inflation can arise, encountered most clearly and distinctly in the various forms of psychosis where the individual merges with an archetypal image and becomes, for example, the Emperor of China or Joan d'Arc. I once experienced a classic example of a complete, but nonpsychotic, identification in the case of a teacher of about forty years of age.

> The patient had grown up in a very narrow sect, a sect that rejected sexuality, regarded it as a sin, and considered it as a necessary evil only within the marriage relationship. It goes without saying that, as in the

Catholic Church, contraception was strictly forbidden. In his midtwenties, he married a woman who came from the same sect, and the couple's circle of friends was made up of sect brothers and sisters. Until he entered analysis with me, he had led a decidedly solid and "pure" life without complications, yet with certain psychosomatic symptoms, particularly involving the stomach and intestines, symptoms which he saw as organic and for which he was constantly in treatment by his internist. Before he called me, some dark premonition that his symptoms might also have something to do with the psyche had guided him to a lecture at a psychoanalytic institute where sexuality was discussed more freely. This struck him, he told me, like a bolt out of the blue, a revelation.

Immediately after the lecture, he visited a brothel for the first time in his life, and there he experienced a more satisfying sexual experience than he had had with his wife. Seized by this knowledge and fired by the inspiration that sexuality was something completely natural and healthy, and that it had to be permitted and expressed in all its forms, he returned home. He began to buy great quantities of sexual literature, got pornographic films, and tried with desperate insistence to convert his wife and circle of friends to experience and live out sexuality in every form, including wife swapping and group sex. (This happened some time before the student revolts of the sixties, and he was, in a sense, a forerunner of this phenomenon that only years later turned into a sort of collective ideology: "If ever you sleep with the same one twice, you've sold your soul at the establishment price.")

Of course, his missionary intentions were a complete failure, and he harvested ugly conflicts, lost friendships, endangered his marriage, and created professional difficulties for himself. A remnant of common sense kept him from disseminating his ideas among his students, but he did attempt to move some of his colleagues in this direction, suggesting at least that they watch his movies.

When he entered analysis with me, he started by uttering a sentence characteristic of his condition: "Herr Doktor, I have painted a penis on my banner!" With this he believed he would win my entire good will and find a comrade-in-arms who, having the right means, could help him persuade his environment and lead him into a new, healthier life. But somewhere in the background he sensed that something in his ideology was not quite right, and he remained in therapy even when, to his deep disappointment, it turned out that it could not help him realize his goals. For a long time this patient's entire ego-complex was, in fact, possessed by his sexual complex, and he spent a long first phase of his analysis incessantly talking about it and also acting on it, so that I often feared for

his social existence. Yet it would have been impossible to call this inflation a psychosis. In the course of subsequent analysis, it turned out that
this "penis on his banner" corresponded to the animus and to the severely repressed sexuality of his vivacious and energetic mother and
was a part object of a positive mother complex that, through the analysis, introduced a transformation in him out of a rigidified and suffocating
elementary character of the Great Mother. The latter was personified in
the narrow regulations and opinions of the collective sect.

5) A further possibility is that the complex is fully unconscious and, via
the defense mechanism of projection, is projected onto the environment.
Here the individual encounters it as a characteristic of some other person or
object. The most frequent of these unconscious projections are the shadow
projections that Jung described in detail in his early work, *The Relations
Between the Ego and the Unconscious* (1934/53). These sorts of shadow
projections play a great role in the genesis of images of the enemy, as I discussed in detail in another work (Dieckmann 1986). According to Jung,
projections can take place only if an appropriate hook is present on which
one can hang them. This hook can be very small, in my experience even so
minute that it is practically nonexistent. Nevertheless a projection can take
place, such as we encounter in the persecutory ideas of the paranoid patient.
The ostensible outer experience is in actuality a hallucinated inner experience projected completely onto the outer world. Here belong also the not-
so-infrequent appearance of spirits and visions that are held to be so real
that many people are as fully convinced of them as they are of the negative
characteristics of the persons onto whom they project their own shadow.

6) Next we should mention the condition in which the complex is known
to consciousness but with only an intellectual awareness while the emotional component remains repressed. This is, of course, only a variation on
partial consciousness in which the patient knows, for example, that he has a
mother complex but cannot resolve it and, moreover, is under its influence
or is ruled by it. We meet this form particularly in patients with the classic
compulsion neuroses who incline toward a rational insight into their complexes as an intellectual defense, which, of course, in no way suffices either
to change their symptoms in the slightest degree or to initiate a process of
individuation. Nowadays this form of defense is widespread and can be
found in all forms of neurosis thanks to the abundance of psychological and
psychoanalytic literature that is available to the lay public in simplified
form. Especially among intellectuals, theories of their own neuroses are a
beloved form of defense. They are often wrong because such theories are
intended to serve as disguises for something else, but yet they also often fit

the description above, and then many patients cannot understand why their deeply held insights do them no good.

An impressive woman patient who I once had in treatment was a sociologist who worked successfully in a large chemical firm and was very intelligent. She was characteristically the father's daughter of a well-known scientist who she idealized and in whom she found not the slightest fault. She had lively and decidedly interesting dreams and brought one or two to each session. Her conscious motivation for analysis with me was that she wanted to learn more about her unconscious in order to become even more successful in her professional development. I suspected that there was a considerable depressive mood lurking in the background, hiding behind what she believed was meant by individuation à la Jung.

Before she entered treatment with me, she had been in therapy with another analyst, with whom she had been quite satisfied and who she had had to leave because her firm offered her a better position in another city. She was clearly a thinking type. Her previous analyst also called himself a Jungian, although he had not qualified as one; rather, he had trained himself through independent study. For a relatively long phase at the beginning of the analytic treatment something remarkable happened: following the initial consultations, the patient began each hour by telling me her dreams, and as soon as she concluded her dream report, she enveloped herself in an expectant silence. She looked at me full of expectation so that I got the impression that I was supposed to take some initial stance vis à vis the content of her dreams.

At first I too remained silent and waited for her associations. This gradually degenerated into a duel of silence of which I had no high opinion, so I began to ask questions about the figures or images that appeared in her dreams. This seemed to irritate the patient even more than my earlier silence. After several hours of this I felt completely helpless and asked her what she hoped to accomplish with her strange behavior since, thanks to her lengthy previous treatment, she must after all know how this process worked. At this she became very annoyed and said that I seemed to her to be a rather unskilled analyst. With my predecessor, the treatment had always started with her telling her dreams. When she had finished, he interpreted the dreams and explained to her both the symbols and the persons appearing in them on the subjective level, using the remainder of the hour to lecture on the symbols and their interconnections. She herself had not needed to say anything more and had taken home a most interesting knowledge of the events taking place in her unconscious. Apparently I was not up to such a task and had not studied Jung sufficiently. She said she was extraordinarily frustrated and furious with me. In my countertransference I noticed quite a bit of anger at the intellectualized arrogance of this woman and her massive defense against a real analytic process, but I realized fairly quickly that this was the powerful and latent aggression against her idealized father who had never been concerned with the real feelings and the real personality of his daughter.

In subsequent hours, it came out that she did have a thoroughly intellectual insight into the problems of her positive father complex, and she even got to the point expressing some criticism at times over what appeared in her dreams. But, unfortunately, her fear of her powerful, latent hate was too great, or my abilities as a relatively young analyst were not sufficient, to take advantage of these opportunities. She decided to end the analysis before we were able to work through this complex. She was able to avoid the pressure of her suffering through her professional successes and her good relationship abilities and thus it was not great enough to force her to come to terms with her problem. We ended the analysis in mutual understanding, and she had at least enough clarity not to seek out a dream interpreter like her first "analyst," an entrepreneur from whom she now expected no help. To this day I am not sure if hers was a premature termination or whether the violent conflict she had with me in that relatively short time might not have been sufficient to help her bring her father down from his pedestal and humanize him.

7) The last possibility to discuss here is the complete, unconscious identity of the ego-complex with a parental figure. This occurs particularly when a patient tries not to become like the parent in question (as Jung has described in his discussion of the mother complex of the daughter). This may seem unlikely—the person in question, after all, consciously applies all of his or her energy to develop other ways of experiencing and behaving. But since the unconscious always stands in a compensatory relationship to consciousness, it usually cancels the conscious intention. Especially in cases of negative parental complexes, this relatively frequent phenomenon usually enters consciousness only late or in the final phase of analysis. After the patient has worked through his or her deep feelings of rage and anger toward the complex figure experienced as malicious or hostile, the patient is in a position to differentiate archetypal projections from the personal figure. Even when the latter has had a very negative and inhibiting effect on the patient's development, the patient can learn to tolerate the shadow aspects as introjects and, in the best of cases, also learn to deal with them in a constructive form.

Usually the first awareness of this problem is painful and unpleasant, but the ego-complex, once stabilized, can bear it and work on it. In this con-nection, I am reminded again of Linda Leonard's (1982) discussion where she describes this process in graphic terms.

In summary, we can reiterate that the seven attitudes of the ego-complex vis à vis the dominant pathological complex fall into three basic groups. The one group is characterized by the ego's unconsciousness of and refusal to recognize the complex. Characteristic of the second group is the projec-tion of the complex to the outer world (noting that projection is a largely unconscious process). The third group embraces the processes of the ego-complex's identification with the complexes, or its identity with them.

There is yet one more attitude the ego-complex can assume: confronta-tion with the complex. Only through confrontation, which we strive for in every analytic process, can we get to the point of having it out with the complex and resolving it. When we dissolve a complex, the psychic energy that was bound in the complex field is released and can flow to other psy-chic realms. It may become available to the ego-complex as disposable, free energy, which the patient often experiences as a distinct increase in available energy with which new activities can be developed. Part of this energy may go to mobilize other complex cores. On the one hand, this gives heretofore neglected or suppressed parts of the soul new life and cre-ates a healthier variety in the complex structure of the psyche. (I describe this process particularly in the chapter where I present a borderline patient and in the accompanying diagrams.) On the other hand, the liberated energy can also lead to a confrontation with another complex within the analytic process. This is especially the case when a father complex overlies a more deeply repressed mother complex with an especially feared archetypal fig-ure at the core, or vice versa.

CHAPTER 4

The Shell of the Complex and the Trigger Situation

To begin this chapter I want to examine the shell of the complex using a clinical example.[1] Of course, I cannot exclude the problems of the core and thus have to take into consideration those core elements that condition the shell. However, in this context, I will otherwise ignore the issue of the core and its personal and archetypal components (I will deal with them in detail in the next chapter on the core of the complex).

Although in the theory of analytical psychology complexes are said to form the basic structure of the psyche, the relevant literature offers no differentiated, thoroughly worked-out clinical example that presents the modus operandi of the core, the shell, and the ego-complex, as well as the dissociation of early developmental components and archetypal components of the complex in their structure and in their details. Jungians generally take it as a rule of thumb that the shell of the complex is composed in part of subjective (personal) associations and in part of objective (archetypal) associations that structure themselves around an archetypal complex core located in the collective unconscious. But rarely discussed is how this structure comes into being through the various developmental phases that mark the process of socialization and later life, and what in consciousness or in the individual's perceptions trigger a particular complex.

It is clear that a complex always consists of a mixture of collective and personal material and that the further its elements are dissociated from the ego-complex, the more mythological the characteristics they take on. Jung described this phenomenon early on and repeatedly in his works on the psychoses (Jung 1907/60, 1914/60, 1919/60, 1958/60).

---

[1]The case vignette discussed in this chapter was first published in *Archetypal Processes in Psychotherapy* (Wilmette: Chiron Clinical Series, Chiron Publications, 1987).

In the following clinical example, which is also a classic neurosis, it is easy to recognize that the mythological and archetypal motifs become ever more distinct as the analysis deepens and the complex core is more intensively penetrated.

My hypothesis here is that very early elements of personal experience get worked into the core of the complex—that is, through a process of progressive dissociation from the conscious ego-complex—and must be taken into account in the structure of the core of the complex. These elements are usually difficult to reconstruct clinically since they lie outside the range of memory in the earliest years of life, but they can be interpolated hypothetically either from specific early experiences (e.g., hospitalizations) or from certain character structures of the parents.

Occasionally it does happen that these sorts of very early experiences can be verified, as the following example from the analysis of a forty-year-old woman patient illustrates,

> This woman had a severe anxiety dream that occurred again and again. In it, she saw a shutter moving in the wind which triggered the most severe anxiety states in her. In waking life, too, she could hardly bear to see shutters flapping in the wind. For a long time during the analysis we were unable to explain this motif until the patient one day had a conversation with her mother. Her mother told her that when she was six months old she was evacuated from Berlin to a small village in the country. One beautiful, sunny day, her mother left her in her cradle on a balcony to go do her grocery shopping. The crown of a tree grew over the balcony, and its leaves gave the baby shade. Suddenly a thunderstorm blew in, and before her mother could get home, it poured. Her mother found her completely distraught, soaked through, and screaming in the cradle. The leafy crown of the tree, swayed by the thunderstorm, corresponded to the shutter.

In recent years, more and more publications have appeared contradicting Freud's notion of the symbolic and fantastic sexual experiences of early childhood. But as public sensitivity to early childhood mistreatment has grown, Freud's earlier theories (he first believed the sexual traumata of his hysterical patients to be historically and literally true) have been rehabilitated (see for example, Williams's "Reconstruction of an Early Seduction" (1988)). We will probably always disagree how much it is a question of a symbolic memory and how much historical event. At different times either may be the case. In the analytic process, it usually cannot be established, and we should guard against tending to one or the other position, as unfortunately many authors today do. What is analytically essential is the way in which these sorts of experienced contents can be worked through and mastered.

Now I would like to take a case example to illustrate how the shell of a complex forms around the core in the course of the process of socialization, and how the complex, or its various parts, are activated and expressed in action by the corresponding trigger.

The patient was a twenty-six-year-old man who consulted me because of a severe anxiety neurosis that made it almost impossible for him to practice his profession as a photographer. He had a number of anxieties of a primarily phobic character. Aside from a diffuse anxiety that something unfortunate might happen, he was afraid to use public transportation and, at every little sign of illness, he developed hypochondriacal anxieties that it might be a serious or fatal illness. Every little pimple on his skin set off his fears of a mortal blood poisoning, and he was afraid of being poisoned by potassium cyanide in his darkroom. His fears had become so strong that six months before commencing analysis, he had admitted himself to a hospital. All his symptoms had developed shortly after he married, approximately nine months before beginning treatment, and without a doubt were connected to his relationship with his wife.

The patient was born shortly before the Second World War began and grew up an only child. Shortly after his birth, his father was drafted and did not return until the patient was five; he spent his early childhood primarily with his mother. His childhood was shaped by turbulent events that, at first glance, present a picture of an extremely endangered childhood. He lived through some of the heavy bombing of Berlin, was evacuated with his mother, but then sent to the country alone when he was still quite young. There he felt so unwell that his mother fetched him back. When he was eleven, his mother died of pneumonia, and his widowed father took over his rearing. His father was very involved in his work, but also had a good emotional relationship with his son, so the patient experienced a period of considerable freedom with his father's support in school and profession up until his marriage. The astonishing thing was that he had almost no memories of his mother; her death as well as the years he spent with her from early childhood up until he was eleven were split off from his consciousness.

Early on in his treatment, it was clear that the patient projected a massive negative mother complex onto his wife. He compared his marriage to Sartre's *Closed Society*; he felt that his wife tormented and plagued him about unimportant things, and he always played the role of the placater. If the tension became too much, he fled the situation and often stayed away from home for hours on end. He experienced his wife as completely domineering in both intellectual and material realms because she came from a better social milieu than he and also earned considerably more in her profession. Accordingly, he relinquished all financial regulation of the household and gave her almost all the money he earned. The entire first phase of his treatment was filled with his descriptions of the marriage from which it was obvious that all the associations to his wife ultimately had a negative character and always included a component that was threatening to him. It became clear that the patient experienced an underlying, unconscious, completely irrational, high-level anxiety around this woman, which evoked, even in minor confrontations between them, psychosomatic symptoms such as trembling hands, increased perspiration, elevated pulse, and so on.

Gradually, in the course of further analysis, he succeeded in approaching the figure of his mother more closely. It came out that she was an intensely compulsive woman who, aside from severe cleanliness and orderliness compulsions, had precisely the same catastrophe anxieties that her son exhibited. All the minutiae of life falling outside the well-established norm triggered strong phobic anxieties in her which, in conjunction with her underlying aggression, led to severe punishment of her son, who was naturally extremely intimidated by his mother's anxieties and who experienced her as decidedly stern and unfeeling. Since his mother had in fact died of pneumonia when he was eleven and had been just as phobic about disease as he was, his experience of her death, which he relived in the analysis, intensified his fears of illness significantly.

The key to his predominant anxiety of being poisoned by potassium cyanide appeared, with a lot of emotion, in about the 120th session. At the age of three, the patient and his mother had gone to the country where relatives had a farm. While playing in the barn, he found two fresh chicken eggs, which he broke open and drank. Full of pride, he told his mother and was confronted with her reaction, which was for him absolutely dreadful and terrifying. First his mother screamed at him and then she gave him a thrashing, after which she lectured him long and hard on how tremendously dangerous it was to eat unwashed eggs and how he could fatally poison himself that way. He was made had to promise solemnly never, ever again to take any unwashed thing into his mouth, let alone eat it.

After recalling this early experience, his fears of potassium cyanide poisoning vanished, and his other anxieties also improved in the course of time as he worked through his identity with his compulsive, overanxious mother. But his fear of his wife, as well by extension of all other women, remained pretty much unchanged although the patient had become aware both rationally and emotionally that he projected his personal negative mother complex to his wife and all other women. Only his identity with the constricting, poisoning, and anxious mother had been relieved, but not his projection onto his wife of the terrible mother.

FIGURE 4.1 Mother

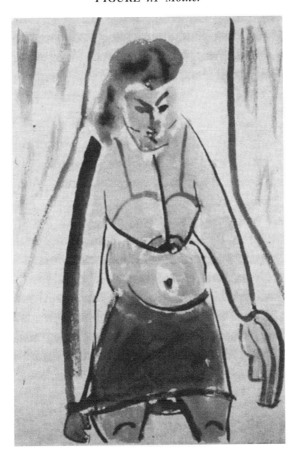

In the course of the next hours, the patient struggled seriously and intensely with this problem. He finally decided, on his own initiative, to draw a picture of this mother, although he was little skilled in drawing. What came out was a figure of a red-haired witch with huge, pointed breasts and an impressive, round belly, wearing a very short, blue skirt (or better, loin cloth), with a powerful, overly large left hand and threatening facial features whose eyebrows were reminiscent of a Mephistopheles (figure 4.1).

This figure had nothing to do with his mother and did not resemble her in the least. She was quite obviously an archetypal figure of the Great Mother with prominent archaic features like those of the Venus of Willendorf. She reminded me most the aggressive mother goddesses such as Ishtar or the Babylonian Tiamat, an impression arising especially from the threatening facial features, the powerful hand, and the mighty, pointed breasts. In his associations she also had some connections to the Great Mother as prostitute, the Great Whore of Babylon (I must also add that he was very much fascinated by prostitutes but had never had any relations with one nor had he ever dared even speak to a prostitute).

His associations to this picture yielded some collective material and some individual, personal material. Among his objective associations, characteristics of the Great Mother in her negative character were prominent. He referred to the woman as an entrapping witch, a depraved whore, and an oppressive death mother. His subjective associations were the blows from his mother's massive hand, which in his painting is depicted as a baseball glove; and although his mother was in fact right-handed, in the picture he painted the left hand as larger than life. The red nipples reminded him of how his mother corrected his homework with red pencil, and he had endured terrible fears about making mistakes.

In this context, he again mentioned the story about the chicken eggs and also recalled an experience from when he was six. He had gotten a scooter as a present, and the first time he tried it, he fell in the street. In so doing he hurt his arm, which led to a questionable case of blood poisoning. He'd had to lie quietly in bed for several weeks and his overanxious mother scrutinized him excessively. This experience, which he had repressed until now, had a subjective individual component, but it was also an experience of the collective, negatively demonic aspect of the world that can, in fact, call forth just such illnesses and poisonings. This was emphasized when the patient was reminded of another early experience: he had witnessed the suicide of a neighbor who threw himself out of the fourth storey of his house to the street below.

Several analytical hours later, the patient brought in a second picture which showed a demonic giant with four arms standing before a cliff watching a tiny figure who has climbed two-thirds of the way to the top (figure 4.2). This giant again has an oversized hand like the mother fig-

FIGURE 4.2 The Holländermichel

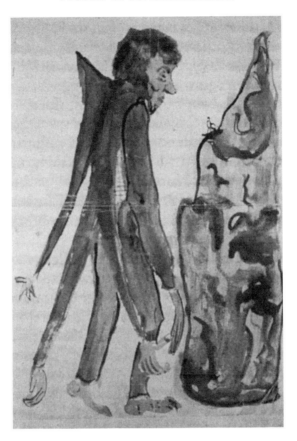

ure, but this time on the right side. The patient named him the Holländermichel, a figure from Hauff's tale, "The Cold Heart" (Hauff 1896).

In this tale, the population of the Black Forest in Swabia is divided into
two groups. One is comprised of the bigger, broad-shouldered woodcutters, and the other of the handsome, serious, and dignified glassmakers.
Each group has its own "spirit" or "daemon": the woodcutters have their
Holländermichel and the glassmakers their Glasmännlein (i.e., glass ho-
munculus). The Glasmännlein is a good spirit, who tends to be associated with the patriarchal realm, while the Holländermichel resembles an
archaic forest demon from the domain of Mother Nature who makes
those who turn to him rich, but in exchange demands their hearts and
replaces them with stones.

In distress, a poor charcoal burner, Peter the Coaler, turns to the Glasmännlein who gives him three wishes. Peter's first wish is to be able to dance so well that he becomes the king of the dance floor, and as his second he asks for the most magnificent glass house and a horse and carriage. The Glasmännlein is annoyed at Peter's stupid wishes and leaves the third unfulfilled. Peter is now rich and king of the dance floor, but he squanders his money and develops a passion for gaming. He finally gambles away everything and is as poor as he was before. The Glasmännlein refuses to help him further.

Peter now turns to the Holländermichel and sells his living heart for 100,000 gulden and a heart of stone. Rich again, he travels around in the world, but soon discovers that he can no longer experience any feelings at all. Finally he asks the Holländermichel to give him back his real heart, but the Holländermichel refuses. Peter becomes the richest and most ruthless businessman in the region. He marries the most beautiful and virtuous maiden in the Black Forest. She is charitable and attempts to help the poor, which enrages the heartless Peter. He kills her with one blow when she gives bread and wine to a poor old man who appears at the door. This old man reveals himself as the Glasmännlein, who curses Peter and threatens to shatter him. But for the sake of Peter's charitable wife, the Glasmännlein gives Peter a week's time in which to mend his ways. In a dream one night, his wife implores him to go once again to the Glasmännlein and demand that his third wish be fulfilled, that is, that he be given back his living heart. The Glasmännlein reveals to Peter how he can trick the Holländermichel to get back his heart. Peter succeeds. When he returns home, his expensive glass house has been struck by lightning and burnt down, and he finds in its place an ordinary peasant house in which his wife is alive and well. From then on, Peter plied his trade undeterred and through his own efforts became prosperous and respected throughout the forest.

In the patient's picture, it is not difficult to tell from the overly large hand, in addition to the motifs of coldness and feelinglessness experienced with his own mother, that we are dealing here with the mother's animus or, more precisely, with a negative, collective animus of the archetypal Great Mother.

In therapy, the patient projected this figure as a positive transference (in Freud's sense) first to me and in subsequent hours was able to bring out his aggression toward authority figures in a personal confrontation for the first time. After repeatedly working through these two pictures, the patient's anxiety disappeared completely, and he was able to experience a very positive inner and outer development. He also succeeded in leaving his hated job as a photo lab assistant to again pursue his real career desires, and he normalized his masochistic relationship in his conflicted marriage. By chance I had the opportunity to see this patient twenty years later, and I found out that the success of the treatment had endured, so in this case, one can speak medically of a cure.

First, I want to diagram the negative mother complex in order to visualize the structure of the complex, showing, on the one hand, the relationships between the core of the complex and the shell and, on the other hand, the relationships between the negative mother complex and the ego complex as the center of consciousness (figure 4.3). (In this depiction, I have left the father complex, which of course plays a role, out of the picture since, in the case of this patient, the mother complex stood prominently in the foreground and introducing the father complex here would go beyond the scope of this chapter. I have also left off discussing the paternal influence on this patient's mother complex.)

Broken line *A* represents the relatively permeable boundary between consciousness and the personal unconscious. As a continual process, contents from the unconscious can rise into consciousness and contents from consciousness can sink into the unconscious. Situated in the center of the field of consciousness, the ego complex, represented as the largest circle, also extends into the unconscious. The unconscious parts of the ego complex would be, for example, the dream ego and the body ego. (Of course, the unconscious parts of the ego would have to extend into the collective unconscious since the possibility of developing the structure of the ego complex depends on archetypal possibilities that extend into the psychoid layers of the objective psyche. But for the sake or clarity, I have not attempted to represent this extension here.)

The smaller circles situated close to the conscious part of the ego complex represent experiences taking place in the here and now that tend to mobilize the complex. Experiences that have a direct connection to the closest personal female relationship (in this case his wife) toward whom his emotions are colored by the complex are included in group 1. In group 2 are those experiences that relate to a wider circle of figures onto whom the negative mother is projected (currently, his mother-in-law). Group 3 embraces the male figures, that is, his authority anxieties (e.g., toward his boss) related to the mother's animus. Group 4 subsumes his experience of the dangerous world environment (e.g., his anxiety of potassium cyanide poisoning in the photo lab).

In the next level, below the threshold of consciousness and situated close to the unconscious part of the ego, i.e., relatively capable of entering conscious, are the influences (groups 1′ through 4′) that lie in the recent past and can be reproduced at any time.

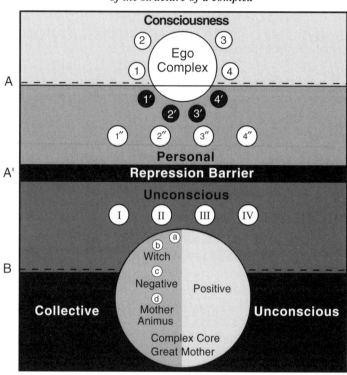

*FIGURE 4.3 The negative mother complex as an example
of the structure of a complex*

Current Anxiety-producing Situations
1 with same-age women, e.g., wife
2 with maternal figures, e.g., mother-in-law
3 with mother's animus, e.g., the Holländermichel
4 impersonal anxieties, e.g., poison

Recent Anxiety-producing Situations
1'–4' current situations that could be made conscious at any time

Older Anxiety-producing Situations Subsequent to the Repression
1" with same-age women, e.g., his first love
2" with older women, e.g., a female teacher
3" with men, e.g., homosexuality
4" with others, e.g., rage attacks when observing others eating fruit

Oldest Anxiety-producing Situations
I   with his own mother, e.g., spankings
II with other women, e.g., child-care workers
III with his father (as mother's deputy)
IV with the environment, e.g., fruit, experiences with "poisoning"

The next lower layer contains experiences that took place in this realm between approximately his eleventh and twentieth years, which are somewhat more difficult to recall but can be fully reproduced. Thus, for example, the experience of a profoundly disappointing love, a girl with whom he began a relationship on a bicycle tour but who then, as he experienced it, rather coldly turned away from him for another, would be included in group 1″. An intimidating woman teacher or an older saleslady who had treated him brusquely would fall into group 2″. In group 3″ would be early partially latent, partially manifest homosexual experiences in which he had played a passive role, likewise associated with the experience of being overwhelmed and anxious. As in all instances of a negative mother complex, latent or partially manifest homosexuality played a considerable role for this patient, too. Finally, group 4″ represents early, anxiety-provoking experiences of the world. Here, for example, belongs the patient's inability ever to eat fruit that had not been carefully washed. When he came to talk about this, he volunteered the information that even now he felt so much envy and rage that he could wring the neck of anybody who pulled an apple out of his pocket and took a delicious bite of it.

Next we have the wide line A' which represents the repression barrier in the personal unconscious formed when he was eleven, following the death of his mother. All complex-colored experiences below this line had been repressed and were made conscious again only during the analytic process. These contents are sorted into groups I through IV.

Group I subsumes his early experiences of being spanked or punished by his mother, for example, the times he licked the lead of a pencil or something similar and his mother dragged him to the sink and scrubbed his tongue. He of course got a spanking in situations of this sort. In group II, we find experiences such as his being evacuated from Berlin to the country where the child-care workers treated him very badly and often spanked him, until he finally wrote his mother asking her to take him back (which she did). Under group III, we would classify another early experience: he had broken his toy fire truck while playing with it. His mother threatened to tell his father, which she did when he came home in the evening; his father then also spanked him. Group IV would include, first of all, his experience of his mother's pneumonia and then her death. One would expect that he would be able to recall this very vividly, but her death and burial and the period immediately following had been completely extinguished from his voluntary memory and was contained under a stable repression barrier.

Next we have the second broken line B representing the transition from the personal to the collective unconscious. Centered in the middle of the collective unconscious we find the core of the mother complex which, unlike the ego complex, rests more in the collective unconscious than in the personal unconscious. Areas in this complex core have been shaded differently to indicate the activation of the core elements, in this case of the negative mother complex. In the upper area of the complex core extending into the personal unconscious, *a* refers to his paranoid experience when he was three of a poisonous world, conditioned by his mother's anxieties when he had eaten the two chicken's eggs. With *b* we designate his falling off his scooter at age six and the real blood poisoning, wherein he experienced Mother Earth's real dangerousness and demonic poisoning in his own body.

These early personal experiences (which we could, of course, discuss in terms of Freud's trauma theory: whether they actually took place literally or whether they represent symbolic formations that depict the child's early intrapsychic situation) are now mobilized in the collective unconscious in the core of the complex as *c* and *d*. In the analysis, these came up in the form of images that represented the collective background figures of this complex: the Witch Mother and Whore, as well as the Holländermichel (as the negative animus of the Great Mother).

Other areas in the core of this complex have been left blank to indicate that there are zones in the core of the mother complex that have not been mobilized in this patient's life history and hence are not populated with corresponding archetypal images. We must imagine this entire two-dimensional representation not only as three-dimensional and in constant motion, but even as four-dimensional, since the individual points have their own particular time. The whole complex is constellated by a trigger event, be it a conflict with his wife, differences with his superior, an encounter with a police person, touching a soiled object, or something of the like, and it is constellated on all levels simultaneously.

This simultaneity of the various temporal levels can be observed empirically in the analytic situation when a complex is activated. In these situations, infantile and adolescent elements are mingled in gesture, pitch of voice, and form of expression. Another interesting component apparent in the constellated complex is the appearance not only of present and past, but also of future (prospective or final) elements. Thus still-unconscious, "more mature" parts of the personality can manifest themselves. In his medical dissertation, "On the Psychology and Pathology of So-Called Occult Phenomena" (1902/57), Jung described a classic example of a complex of this sort that clearly contained significant aspects of a potentially more mature personality.

In respect to the strength of the complex vis à vis the ego complex, we can clearly differentiate two situations. In the first, the complex is activated, and the corresponding phenomena such as tensions, anxieties, Freudian slips, etc., occur, but the executive function of the ego is preserved so that the individual remains in a position to behave in a relatively well-adapted and rational manner. In terms of our patient, this would be the case, for example, if he met a policeman on the street, sensed his own tension and anxiety, but was still able to pass by and continue on his way. In the second situation, so much energy is activated in the complex that it overrides the ego's executive function and the individual is no longer capable of reacting ego-syntonically. The ego is overwhelmed by the complex and the complex reacts in place of the ego. Jung characterized this situation aptly: "Everyone knows nowadays that people 'have complexes.' What is not so well known, though far more important theoretically, is that complexes can *have us*" (1948/60a, par. 200). A Jewish patient once described to me very impressively how strong this sort of complex reaction can be:

> While driving to her session, she encountered a motorcyclist who was weaving back and forth among the cars. She attempted to avoid him, somewhat anxiously, and the motorcyclist obviously felt she was holding him back. When they both had to stop at a traffic light and were sitting next to each other, he shouted some bad-tempered words at her. She could not understand the content since her window was closed, but she could see from his facial expression that he was threatening her. The patient was thrown into an exceptional frame of mind: the entire street in front of her nearly disappeared before her very eyes, and she suffered a powerful anxiety attack. Only with difficulty was she able to get through the intersection and pull up to the curb, where she had to park for five to ten minutes, shaking all over, until gradually she regained some degree of calm and was able to drive on.

> Later we were able to reconstruct the background of this experience in her session. The patient had a massive negative father complex. Both parents had been in concentration camps during the war, which they had survived. Their marriage following the war had been unhappy from the beginning, and they divorced when she was four. The patient grew up with her mother, who, for her part, cast the father and his entire family in the role of devils. All good came from the maternal side, from the mother's family, and everything mean and evil from the paternal. She spent her first four, relatively happy, childhood years in Israel; then she came with her mother to Germany where she was held captive in a room, not even permitted to look out the window because her mother feared that her father could kidnap her. Combining this situation and the brutal concentration camp experiences of her Jewish family (of whom only a few had survived the National Socialist massacre), Germany became, for this patient, an absolutely negative, demonic "Fatherland" in the archetypal sense, although neither parent was born German. This patient also experienced a distinct sense of liberation whenever she crossed the German border, and many of the anxieties and feelings of confinement she experienced in Germany fell away. Germany as a

whole had, for her, the symbolic character of a concentration camp, of being confined in a narrow space where she constantly had to fear that something horrible would happen. The motorcyclist turned into an SS trooper whose displeasure constellated in her a mortal fear and, in the background, her violent but latent aggression.

In the first situation described, where the executive function of the ego is maintained, it has been my experience that only those forms of experience associated to the particular trigger stimulus are mobilized, but not the entire complex. It was easy to observe this in the case of the patient discussed in detail above. When he brought in his second picture, the one of the Holländermichel, and projected this figure onto me, his associations were always only of events connected to male authorities, homoerotic and homosexual tendencies, and memories linked to his father as mother's animus. Thus the system mobilized (3, 3', 3", and III in the diagram) is designated in the core of the complex as the mother's animus. The situation was different when the Witch was constellated, since the associations around this image, which had caused him significantly greater anxieties, related to all four levels. The energy intensity that tends to manifest in this instance is, in many cases, astonishing, since it frequently far exceeds the psychic libido quantum normally available to the individual. It resembles what we often observe in extraordinary circumstances: the individual can command energy quanta for short periods of time that seemed impossible and with which "superhuman" accomplishments are possible. It is clearly the case that we have available to us in the collective unconscious a reserve of energy, a sort of dormant energy, that cannot be mobilized by acts of will, but that can be released via a complex reaction, whether in a constructive or destructive manner.

In conclusion, I would like to discuss a question that seems to me important as a hypothesis although unanswerable as yet. Specifically, when a complex is constellated, are we dealing with a causal nexus or with an authentic synchronistic activation of the qualities of experience at various levels?

If it should be the case that the synchronicity principle plays a significant role in the mobilization of a complex, this bridges another important fact, namely, that complexes as a rule constellate not only "inside" but also "outside," and their psychic energies transcend the individual. Such energies play a considerable role when these sorts of complexes are mobilized in the transference-countertransference situation in analysis, where they may lead to clusterings of apparently parapsychological phenomena, such as the Berlin group described in its studies (Dieckmann 1971; Blomeyer 1971).

We could imagine a causal chain such that a trigger event, for example, a present-time encounter with an authority figure (3), activates relatively current experiences with the same authority figure (3′), the early adolescent experiences up to age eleven (3″), and ultimately the early childhood experiences of the father and, in the core of the complex, of the mother's animus (III). Synchronicity would mean that no causal relationship obtains; rather, all the realms of experience in group 3 or, in the extreme case, even all the qualities listed here (since they are all interrelated) are activated without any temporal delay.

In modern physics, there is a phenomenon that we could take as a metaphor for this sort of event: the EPR experiment and Bell's theorem (von Franz 1992). Electrons have a "spin" such that a particle can "rotate" in either direction around its axis. Only when one performs an experiment to establish a given axis of rotation can one determine that the electron spins in the one or the other direction. This means that the particle assumes a specific axis of rotation in the instant that one measures it whereas previously it had only a tendency or a potential to so. In the EPR experiment, two electrons are spun in opposite directions. These two electrons are widely separated from one another; the distances may be as great as one wishes, say from Berlin to New York or to the moon. The quantum theory states that in a system of two particles whose total spin equals zero, the spin of the two particles around all possible axes must always be in opposite directions even though the actual spin of the particles prior to measurement exists only as a tendency or possibility. What is paradoxical in this experiment is the observer's freedom to chose the axis to be measured. As soon as the observer chooses, the act of measuring transforms the tendency of the particles to rotate about a certain axis into a certainty. The axis of measurement can be chosen when the two particles are already at a great distance from each other. But as soon as we have measured the first particle, the second particle will assume a definite spin—up or down if we chose a vertical axis, left or right if we chose a horizontal axis—even when they are thousands of miles apart. This happens at the same instant since, according to Bohr, the two-particle system constitutes an indivisible totality even if the particles are separated by great distance. Although widely separated in space, they are bound in an immediate, nonlocal relationship, phenomena that transcend our conventional concepts of information transmission.

Metaphorically speaking, our system of complexes might be similar. Although the condensed data of experience belong to different time periods and lie at different levels of consciousness and the unconscious, they are at the same time an indivisible whole and react accordingly. Of course, I am only offering an hypothesis here, since we lack the possibility of monitoring or measuring the transmission of information and the quantities of libido in psychic events. Nevertheless, this hypothesis increases in probability when we consider how, especially in conditions highly charged with affect (as happens when complexes are constellated), synchronistic events transpire more frequently and can be observed in the surroundings of the person concerned. According to Jung's (1956/63) later insights (in the sense of the *unus mundus* hypotheses) and Erich Neumann's conception of the unitary reality (1959/89), the activation of the archetypal energies creates constellations that reach beyond the individual.

CHAPTER 5

The Core of
the Complex

Before we turn to the structure of the core of the complex and its problems, it is important to reconsider an issue that Jung brought up early on when he distinguished two different sorts of complexes: one group originating in the personal unconscious, and another group whose core was to be found in the archetypal realm. It therefore seems sensible to present a quick overview of the development of the positions we find in Jung's writings.

It is well known that Jung was occupied with the association experiment for many years following his discovery of the feeling-toned complex. In this connection, he states in several places (1902/57, 1948/60a) that complexes are contents of the personal unconscious whereas the content of the collective unconscious consists of archetypes. (This early conception still haunts the literature and was even taken over in this form, for example, by Velikowsky (1982) in his book, *Das kollektive Vergessen*.) But these statements of Jung's do not agree with what he writes in other places: that there are two different categories of complexes, of which the one is created on the basis of personal experiences in the individual's life while the other consists of complexes that were never before conscious and therefore could not have been repressed. These complexes arise from the collective unconscious, and at certain threshold situations in psychic life they function to facilitate a different, new attitude of consciousness and contain irrational contents of which the individual has never before been conscious. Jung mentions these collective complexes in his 1948 essay, "On Psychic Energy" (1948/60b), and draws a parallel with primal peoples' belief in souls and spirits. Jung clearly differentiates these two categories of complexes in another essay, "The Psychological Foundation of Belief in Spirits" (1948/60a), where he distinguishes primal peoples' experiences of "loss of soul" from "possession" by a spirit. The complexes of the personal unconscious, which, among other things, arise from early traumatic experiences or from certain familial structures and atmospheres in early childhood, are as a rule subject to repression. Of course, the ego-complex experiences this splitting off of a complex from the personal unconscious as a loss of libido, and since the split-off complex is emotionally charged, it does not lose its activity. This corresponds to what primal peoples call "loss of soul." If one succeeds in dissolving this sort of complex, or in making its content again accessible to consciousness, the individual experiences a considerable degree of relief and, thanks to the increase in libido, the feeling of enhanced psychic energy.

The situation is profoundly different with those complexes that originate in the collective unconscious and are filled primarily with irrational, mythological contents. The eruption of this sort of complex from the collective unconscious is often an exceedingly unpleasant, even dangerous, event for consciousness. These complexes manifest when an external threat has made a deep impression on an individual such that the individual's usual attitude to life threatens to collapse or when the contents of the collective unconscious have such great energy that they erupt into consciousness like a foreign spirit or demon. Since Jung always started with the healthy structure of the psyche and emphasized the prospective significance of the activity of the human unconscious, he did not regard the complexes originating in the collective unconscious as basically pathological; rather, they contained in their mythological symbols the beginnings of and possibilities for a fundamental transformation of consciousness. This will become clearer in subsequent chapters as I illustrate my points with appropriate case examples.

In the course of my analytic practice, doubts have gradually arisen as to whether this division between types of complexes (that is, those of the personal unconscious and those of the collective unconscious) can be sustained, although it is still used by many Jungians (Seifert 1981). Already in his forward to J. Jacobi's 1940 text, *Die Psychologie von C. G. Jung,* Jung (1939) makes a connection between a complex of the personal unconscious and of the collective unconscious. In that forward, he expresses the opinion that complexes rest on "typical foundations" that correspond to an emotional readiness or, to be precise, the instincts. These residues of the instincts express themselves in human beings in two ways: they have a dynamic aspect (that is, a relatively high charge of drive energy) and a formal side. The formal aspects (one could also say "spiritual") of the instincts express themselves in human beings in unreflected, involuntary fantasy images which, for their part, take up large parts of our inner world and evoke specific attitudes and actions. It is here that we trace a direct connection between the complex that expresses itself in the personal unconscious as an acquisition in the life of the individual and a deeper basis that is anchored in the archetypes of the collective unconscious. Williams (1988) expressed this thought more incisively when she wrote of an "indivisibility of the collective and personal unconscious" and then pointed out that personal elements always occur in conjunction with the collective unconscious whence they gain their relation to consciousness and, vice versa, collective contents are contained in the personal unconscious that provide the strong, anxiety-laden quantities of energy. However, she makes her statements about the collective and the personal unconscious in general terms and does not refer expressly to the difference between the core and the shell of the complex.

In the work of Jung's old age, *Mysterium Coniunctionis* (1956/63), this idea of the relation of the core of the complex to the conscious ego-complex appears again. The ego-complex as the aging, weakened King Sol is in need of renewal, of an ever-repeated renewal in the course of the individuation process. Usually there is already an unconscious connection to a complex with archetypal foundations that is in a position to bring forward the new spiritual contents, to effect the renewal of the dynamic forces, and to dethrone the aging as it becomes conscious. Since complexes, as extraordinarily differentiated structures in the human psyche, present sort of part personalities, Jung ascribes to them a certain luminosity which is capable of becoming conscious, whereby he expresses the idea that the dominants of consciousness which have become weakened with age can also be renewed and strengthened by these "secondary lights" that already contain a kind of consciousness or possibility of consciousness.

It is clear that a complex always consists of a mixture of collective and personal material, and the farther its parts are dissociated from the ego complex, the more mythological the character they take on. Here I am advancing the hypothesis that even in the core of the complex—even in the case of a great dissociation from the ego-complex—elements of very early personal experience are enmeshed and must be taken into account in the structure of the core. For the most part, it is difficult to reconstruct them clinically since they lie outside the realm of voluntary recall in the very earliest periods of life. But they can be hypothetically included with a degree of probability bordering on certainty either on the basis of specific early experiences (for example, the very early birth of a younger sibling or a hospitalization) or according to the character structure of the parents.

In the following, I will first present a clinical example. In the analysis, four complexes existed side by side, initially appearing to be very different. But it is not a very complicated matter to situate these four different complexes in the basic complex structure I described earlier.

In the various phases of the analysis, one or another of the complexes always tended to occupy the foreground, although of course all were present concurrently. First and foremost, I was dealing with the complex of a radiant, Apollonian father god, an all-powerful, highly revered figure who determined the life of the patient, a woman, and kept her completely dependent.

If we adapt Jung's pyramidal schema of this all-powerful father god

(Jung 1959) to the modified model I am proposing, initially the result would be this pattern: at the topmost point of the first pyramid, where Jung placed the Apollonian deity, we would situate the positive father figure. (Here I must note that, in his pyramidal schema, Jung attempted to outline the Self, whereas initially I am attempting to conceptualize—in the sense of a general theory of the neuroses, based on the complexes—the two great complexes of the archetypal father and the archetypal mother, which I will later incorporate into Jung's schema.)

The Apollonian father represented in a pyramidal schema would have to look like figure 5.1.

Before I continue the case presentation, I must comment on the pyramidal schemata representing the father and mother archetypes. I have altered these in accordance to the diagnosis of complexes, and I have not given the mythological and biblical names that Jung uses, particularly for the top pyramid. Likewise, the tension between Christ and the Devil is absent; I will address this later when I discuss the Self.

In the top pyramid, intended to represent the various forms in which the father archetype manifests, we see at the apex the image of God, which, in our conception, the child's psyche projects to the personal father. In the case being discussed here, the father was an Apollonian god of the highest degree of purity and radiant consciousness. In other cases, it may not be an Apollonian god who occupies that supreme position, but instead the figure of a Zeus, a Dionysus, an Aries, or a Hephaestus. Pluto, too, as the god of money takes his place here not infrequently. So many differentiated figures populate the Greek pantheon that we can usually find in one or another of them the idealizations to which a patient falls victim when he or she worships a deity. In this manner, we can rather quickly establish some level of diagnosis of the highest values a given patient attempts to follow.

Let us return momentarily to our patient with her Apollonian god image and attempt to trace the other complexes that also populated her psyche. A second complex existing in this patient had as its core element the archetypal image of a depraved old man with murderous aggression, a split that we also find frequently in patients with borderline characteristics. This would be the negative senex complex, which we situate on the shadow side of the second pyramid, above and to the left.

The patient found herself in perpetual flight from this negative senex, not only in waking life but in her dreams, where he pursued her with instruments of murder. With his characteristics of Dionysian debauchery, he was obviously the counterpole to the Apollonian, pure, noble, ordering deity. The Apollonian deity caused in my patient significant compulsive traits that found expression in exaggerated cleanliness, immaculate clothing, and scrupulous domestic tidiness. The negative senex complex, in con-

FIGURE 5.1 Structure of the Father Archetype

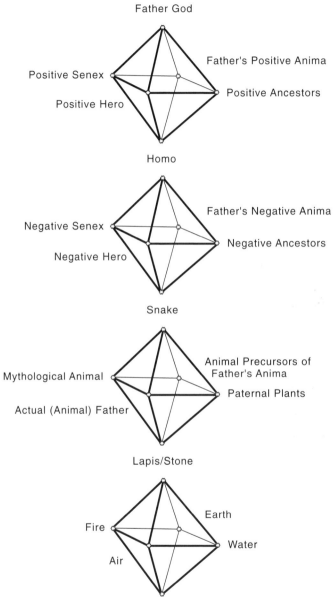

Father God

Father's Positive Anima

Positive Senex

Positive Ancestors

Positive Hero

Homo

Father's Negative Anima

Negative Senex

Negative Ancestors

Negative Hero

Snake

Animal Precursors of
Father's Anima

Mythological Animal

Paternal Plants

Actual (Animal) Father

Lapis/Stone

Earth

Fire

Water

Air

Rotundum/Great Round as the Sun

FIGURE 5.2 Structure of the Mother Archetype

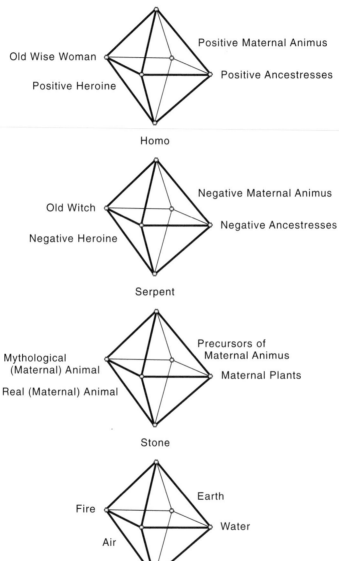

Mother Goddess

Positive Maternal Animus

Old Wise Woman

Positive Ancestresses

Positive Heroine

Homo

Negative Maternal Animus

Old Witch

Negative Ancestresses

Negative Heroine

Serpent

Precursors of
Maternal Animus

Mythological
(Maternal) Animal

Maternal Plants

Real (Maternal) Animal

Stone

Earth

Fire

Water

Air

Great Round as the Moon

trast, was characterized by alcoholism, dependency on pills, and impersonal liaisons with men.

A third complex corresponded to a puella, with all of the typical immaturity that Linda Leonard (1982) depicts so fully in her figure of the beauty. In this case, we could designate this as a persona complex, behind which was concealed a fourth complex, namely that of a helpless little girl.

In my further elaborations, I will attempt to subsume the patient's four primary complexes under the core element of the ambivalent father complex and, at the same time, develop my notion of the structure of the core of the complex. Additionally, I would like to note that, just as I have explained in regard to the Apollonian deity, the negative senex can appear in distinctly varied forms. For example, it can resemble an overly stern grand inquisitor, as E. Jung (1971) has pointed out, or it can be an old drinking buddy or a false prophet who leads youth astray, and more of the like. The same holds true for the beauty or the helpless child. Everywhere there are diverse variants of the several types, which is exactly what brings about the individual quality of each human being and makes it impossible to force anyone into a simple schema such as at first glance might appear to be possible in the pyramidal diagram of the father and mother complexes.

Now I would like to sketch the clinical picture of this patient.

The patient was a young woman, age 24, who suffered from mildly paranoid fantasies of being followed, severe anxiety states, and a whole series of compulsive actions and ideas, as well as psychosomatic symptoms, particularly in the gastrointestinal tract. By and large, she was close to the edge of a hysterical psychosis.

An intense father-daughter bond was characteristic; she was decidedly a father's daughter with a clearly positive and also mildly eroticized father complex. The father himself came from a family of academicians and had chosen the life of an academic, in which he was very successful. He had married the daughter of a well-to-do businessman and had had three children, of whom the patient was the oldest. Following her, the two sisters were born rather close together. From her birth on, she was the favorite of her father, with whom she had an extremely close relationship and with whom she made a number of trips even when she was older. According to my patient's experience, her mother was very beautiful but also an emotionally cool woman. She placed great value on the external and obviously had strong compulsive characteristics. The two younger sisters inclined more toward their mother, whereas a cool impersonality, reserve, and, in part, strong rejection predominated between the patient and her mother.

Corresponding to her fixation on her father, at the tender age of seventeen the patient had married a man her father's age who was one of her father's scholarly colleagues and a frequent visitor in their home. The young woman's marriage was unhappy. Early on, my scrupulously honest patient was forced to recognize that the husband she idealized, as she had her father, had some downright dishonest characteristics: he falsified the results of his scientific work, ruthlessly exploited his students for his own investigations, and more. Moreover, he suffered from a sexual perversion of a voyeuristic and exhibitionistic nature.

Since, as is well known, we tend to be permissive with those we view as gods, my patient bore this situation for five years, but she became more and more depressive, compulsive, and paranoid. When she finally refused to continue his sexual practices, they divorced. She had borne a child, a son, during the second year of the marriage, who was placed with her after the divorce. At first, he lived with her, and she attempted to rear him. Unfortunately, she was totally dependent on her ex-husband's irregular support payments, and he moreover tried all sorts of tricks, often successfully, to interrupt payment. At times, she was totally without any money. She had left secondary school before graduating, had no job training, and was soon in an untenable position. She knew no better recourse than to turn to older men as father figures and let them support her in order to maintain the relatively costly life style to which she was accustomed. Since she was a very attractive woman with her own individual style, it was not especially difficult to find men of adequate means and to start affairs with them. Unfortunately, these men were usually married and not willing or in a position to forsake their marriages, so these affairs never lasted very long.

In time, her family, who lived in another city, found out about the change in their daughter's way of life, and they initially renounced her rather harshly. At that time, her neurosis worsened, particularly in relation to her powerful, free-floating anxieties, so that she was no longer able to care for her child, now five years old. In a panic reaction, she voluntarily relinquished him to her ex-husband, who had sought custody all along.

Not long after, the ex-husband became seriously and chronically ill so that he could no longer keep his son. My patient had no other option than to take her son back with her in her one-room apartment. But he had grown into a physically active child; she was no longer a match for him and sent him to live with distant friends.

At the intervention of a current fatherly friend, she decided finally to do something about her increasingly neurotic anxiety symptoms. She realized that she could not go on living as she had been. She was so severely regressed that she was not even able to look for a therapist. Hence, her friend made the first appointment for her with me.

In the first phase of her therapy, this friend always drove her to her sessions in his car, waited outside for her until she was done, and then took her home again, although he had rather demanding professional commitments of his own. During this time, the patient became so restricted in practical matters that she could not leave her flat at all except when accompanied by another person. When she did venture out, paranoid feelings and images of being delivered over to a completely hostile world played a large role.

When she came to me for the first time, she appeared in especially pretty, endearing, and somewhat childish attire. The compulsive element was especially evident: all the colors were strictly coordinated; there wasn't a wrinkle in her clothing; nothing was askew; except that everything was just a bit too exact, too much the little daughter wanting to please the father.

In the transference, it was obvious that she saw a father figure in me, and she behaved accordingly. It was also impossible to overlook the strong erotic tone of the transference and the clear, but at first unconscious, wish to seduce me. On the other hand, this was colored by the most severe incest anxieties and probably by fears of perverse practices such as she had experienced with her husband. Only much later in the analysis did she confess to me the background of these fears. They had to do with a compulsive image that she had experienced nightly: shortly after engaging in sexual relations with her husband, and also subsequently with all her older men friends, she regularly awakened in the middle of the night and experienced a very powerful impulse to run to the kitchen, fetch a sharp butcher knife, and stab her sleeping partner. Sometimes this impulse had been so powerful that she was not able to fall asleep again for a long time and lay awake trembling next to her lover.

It was characteristic of this patient to continue to project the positive component of the father archetype, unchanged, to her father, even after he had rejected her, while the negative pole was displaced to her husband or, later, to her older male friends, following the honeymoon of new love. Clearly this practiced displacement was closely linked with consummated sexuality and the aggression that penetration by these men released in her.

Thus we can establish that, for this patient, we were dealing with a positive father complex that carried the pure and compulsive characteristics of an Apollonian god. As a consequence of this compulsivity and her ever-present repetition compulsions, she was captive to a situation that prevented the possibility of developing her personality in the sense of individuating. Here we could speak of imprisonment in the negative elementary character of the father, parallel to what Neumann (1955) calls captivity in the negative elementary character of the mother.

It is not rare to encounter a deified father when working with a woman patient. But this patient was exemplary in exhibiting this phenomenon. First of all, the father was identical with a god insofar as that is possible from the standpoint of the unconscious, and she was firmly convinced of his immortality. The same was the case with her husband and in her transference to me. She showed me letters that she had written to her husband shortly after her marriage. In them, she worshiped him as an all-powerful and omniscient god. As with her father, he corresponded to an Apollonian figure from Greek mythology. He was a god of clarity, of boundless knowledge, a god of truth and of justice, and simultaneously a god of the muses and of artistic creativity. Onto this man she projected an image that corresponded to the best qualities of her father but completely excluded the shadow aspects.

The well-known psychic law of "all or nothing," or the active splitting that Kernberg (1975) describes so well, became active in her only long after the marriage when she was no longer able to overlook her husband's shadow aspects. From that moment on, he became a dark, depraved, old, repulsive figure. At the same time, he was a wicked dictator, a dark, negative principle that pursued her in terrifying nightmares. The only way she was able to defend herself against this devilish figure was to plunge a knife into him as she had in her compulsive fantasies and phobias, an image from the world of impulse that, of course, terrified and tortured her.

The first dream following the reversal of her compulsive impulse (which was, of course, foreign and ego-dystonic) corresponded to the image of the death-dealing, negative senex: "I am in flight from an old man who pursues me with an axe. When he realizes that he cannot catch up with me, he gets a bow from somewhere and shoots an arrow at me. Thank God, it just misses me, and I can find safety behind the shoulder of a cliff."

This is not an unusual dream for women who are pursued by fear of the masculine, but here it is clear that in this senex we are confronted at an archetypal level by an old man with the features of the "far-shooting" Apollo, the god who, with his terrible and far-reaching arrows, kills all the children of Niobe. Kindly Providence, in this case hiding behind an outcropping of a cliff which we could regard as the analysis, saves the patient from a sorry fate.

Although she was in fact quite good looking, my patient experienced herself as ugly and unattractive. The beautiful woman in the family was her mother (also a puella figure) who shone at all social functions and always collected a crowd of admirers around her with whom she held court. The following dream shows very clearly the patient's attitude toward and experience of her mother. She brought this dream in approximately the thirtieth hour of analysis:

> I am in a foreign city and am visiting a certain house; I am supposed to be there and have been invited. Finally I find it. When I ring the doorbell, an elegant and beautiful woman between forty and fifty opens the door. She looks at me, surprised and displeased, and asks what I want. Meanwhile I have forgotten everything and no longer know what I am doing here and stammer out some apology. Then this woman slams the door in my face. It begins to rain and gets colder and colder. I feel totally lonely and abandoned and wake up bathed in tears.

During the hour in which she reported this dream, the patient talked about her hopeless relationship to her mother in which she had never experienced warmth, closeness, or tenderness. Mother, she said, had actually been only a trophy for her father, a beautiful wife for her father's social and academic responsibilities. Not until late in the analysis did she mention that her two younger sisters had experienced their mother quite differently. With them, their mother had been much more related and human, and she had often played with all three of her daughters. For my patient, however, her mother remained impersonal, actually only an archetypal figure as the father's anima. In her experience, she had existed only through, for, and above him.

When we summarize the core of this positive father complex in the initial phase of the analysis, we find the following features:

1) the imago of a positive, Apollonian father god;
2) early and later positive experiences of the personal father (being his favorite daughter, taking trips together, the incestuous eros, etc.);
3) projection of the father's archetypal shadow, in the form of the negative senex, onto other men;
4) the beautiful puella mother as the father's positive anima;
5) the rejecting, unrelated, cold, and ruthless mother figure (as described in the dream above) as the father's negative anima.

If we now return to the pyramidal schema, we can diagram the positive image of the father in the first, topmost pyramid, which, as discussed earlier in detail, includes the very early personal experiences of the human father. Earlier I presented the theoretical rationale in detail and therefore conceptualize Homo, not only as an archetypal figure but also as the personal father and the patient's early experiences of him, whether real or fantasied, under the lower pole of the pyramid (see figure 5.3).

FIGURE 5.3

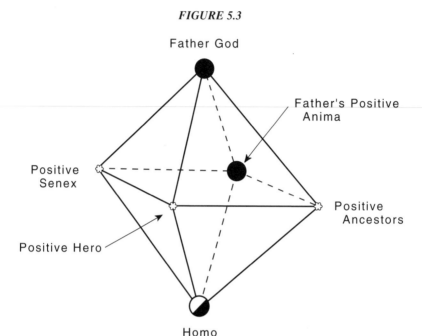

The core elements of the complex that belong to the positive father figure (heavy black circles) are activated and consequently determine the patient's behavior and quality of experience, as described in chapter 4. We have already elaborated what an important position the complex of the Apollonian god was for her. The next activated complex core is that of the father's positive anima, which the patient attempted to function as in her mother's stead. This complex also accounts for her positive, friendly, and adaptive puella attitude through which she attracted men, especially older men, who projected their anima onto the relative emptiness of the puella, as E. Harding (1948) has described. The last is that of the human father. (The half black circle representing it is intended to indicate that the patient saw and experienced only the positive side.) Here belong all the positive experiences that she had had with her father from earliest childhood on.

The three remaining positions on the pyramid remained completely uncathected. She knew absolutely nothing of her ancestors and her family did not talk about them, so of course she could not experience any of them as either positive or negative figures with which to identify. Certainly in her experience of her father, he was not a positive senex figure since her relationship to him never included the qualities that corresponded to such a figure and there never developed between father and daughter the relationship of trust in which a father supports and furthers the development of a daughter's personality and individuation. Just like her mother, the patient served more as a piece of ornamentation (in her experience, at least) and as a subordinate who unconditionally obeyed the father god.

Likewise, we must leave the hero complex open. For all his academic success, she portrayed her father as an anxious man who never held an unconventional opinion of his own, but rather, like many professors, worked his way up the academic ladder honestly if unimaginatively as a "company man." Characteristically, soon after attaining his professorship, his publications diminished markedly, and he devoted himself to teaching and bureaucratic activities.

Now let us look at the shadow side, that is, the second part of the pyramid, represented in figure 5.4. Again, the dark circles indicate the corresponding activated core elements.

On the shadow side of the father complex, we see that only one core is mobilized for this patient. This is the negative senex, which I described

FIGURE 5.4

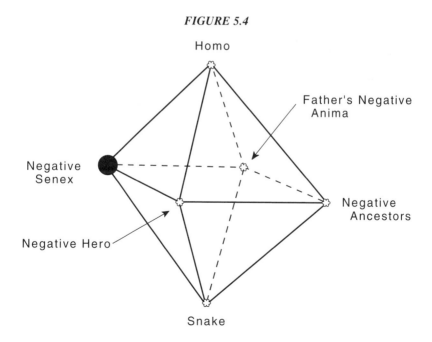

Homo

Father's Negative
Anima

Negative
Senex

Negative
Ancestors

Negative Hero

Snake

in detail in her clinical history. Naturally, we have to add here that in actuality she always sought the senex as a positive figure; but as a consequence of not having it out with her father's shadow (which I left uncircled in this schema to indicate that neither did she perceive it nor was it activated as a core element in the complex), she always fell victim to it.

Ideally, in a moderately healthy person one would expect all the core elements of the father complex to be cathected to a greater or lesser degree. In this sense, these pyramids also show a therapeutic concept in that one could aim at activating more complex core elements and associating them with the ego-complex. Then the ego-complex could draw on their various possibilities in relevant situations, which only then makes the plasticity of life into a living totality.

In these two schemata, I have attempted to comprehend all those great anthropomorphic figures that constitute the core of the father complex. (The animal, vegetable, and elemental domains belong in the lower pyramids, and I will deal with them at the end of this chapter.) Now I would like to discuss the various core elements somewhat more closely. I am taking for granted that the pantheon, the anima, and the ancestors are sufficiently well known. Their manifestations in literature and in analytical psychology, as well as in mythology, have been described often, and one can easily read about them there.

The situation is different with the figure of the senex. By senex I mean not only the figure of the old wise man in his various forms. Here we must include the figure of the just judge, the experienced teacher, the tolerant and mature personality of a man, the white, that is, positive magician, or simply the figure of the calm observer. This is not a complete list but only gives the reader a glimpse of the possibilities.

The figure of the hero has been extensively discussed in the literature, as, for example, by Campbell in *The Hero with a Thousand Faces* (1949). We should add that it is not only the cultural hero that Jung mentions, but also the hero of simple strength, daring, and ability such as we find in modern athletes who often are figures with whom youths identify. Of course, one can object that youthful heroes are not fathers. But just as the young king arises from the dying old king, the youthful hero is shaped by the father. (Our only alternative would be to rename the basic complexes in masculine and feminine terms, but because of the general prevalence of the terms *father complex* and *mother complex*, I have not done so.)

The negative hero subsumes not only the father figures whose lives fail or whose dreams of success exist only in fantasy (as in, for example, Arthur Miller's *Death of a Salesman*), but also the men who fall ill or become addicted without coming to terms with these realities. Similarly, we can count the *petit bourgeois*, the henpecked husband, and the coward among this number. Younger contemporary figures belonging in this company are the temporarily successful drug dealer and the insolent yuppie.

In the vicinity of the negative senex we find, first of all, the dark, black magician, the false prophet, the negative dictator, tyrant, or grand inquisitor. To all these examples—as well as those from the other areas—we can add additional representatives according to the pattern of the archetypal, historical, mythological, or ethnological figures that appear.

This abundance of possibilities in the core of the complex—or, in other words, the imagos in this core—corresponds again to the individuality of the human being. From the point of view of the principle of individuation, we do not imply reducing all to one, or homogenization. Rather, diversity imparts to the individual a unique destiny and personality. It also enables the analyst to come to terms in fantasy with these images and emotions in the transference/countertransference process. On the other hand, subsuming the abundant possibilities under the supraordinate concepts I have suggested prevents us from getting lost in vagueness and loose ends. We are better able to hold on to the main thread of the analytic process. Especially for the beginner and the student, this has the advantage of making it possible to establish a diagnosis in terms of complexes in the initial phase of analysis that does not rest on arbitrary fantasies. Such a diagnosis rests on the patient's psychic material, to which the transference and countertransference constellation can be related. What is the value, for example, of diagnosing the patient in the case above as having "an erotic complex," something we often hear from colleagues? Fundamentally, this tells us nothing at all and completely fails to grasp the unconscious background, unlike a diagnosis in terms of a specific father complex, such as we are suggesting. It has been my experience, personally as well as with candidates in training, that this kind of highly differentiated diagnosis is often possible as early as the first interview (Dieckmann 1991), although it is more valuable and more certain to know a patient over several hours during the initial phase.

We need not say much more about the ancestors on the righthand side of the pyramid. They are the shadow figures or the scapegoats in the family history, and they carry all the negative material that does not correspond to the collective ethical norms and images of the family. In many cases, however, they can exert a decided fascination on the patient, as was the case with the *Schinderhannes* I described in chapter 1. Identifications not infrequently happen here that by no means always have to be negative since, as we know, the shadow also contains values that can help the personality gain greater vitality and richness in life. One impediment often lies in the family's latent or even manifest fear that the child could be heir to an inferior ancestor and come to resemble him or her. This might be an ancestor with a physically or psychologically impaired personality, an inferior character, or even a criminal. Of course, virtually every family has a skeleton in the cupboard. As a rule, so much additional archetypal material is woven about this person in the family legends that the personal and the collective unconscious elements are intricately intertwined.

Naturally, the same holds true for the positive ancestors (in the first pyramid). There we find the leading personalities, say a particularly learned man, a famous academic, or an artist, a successful politician, or the like. Here we encounter again and again the phenomenon Jung described in many places as the "divine parents," that is, a second, "higher" parental couple from whom the child (in fantasy) actually descended and who, as in the case of the Greek demigods, determine the child's destiny. (I have described this phenomenon in detail in my works on Rainer Maria Rilke (Dieckmann 1981a) and Gauguin (Dieckmann 1981b).)

In regard to the father's negative anima, I have already pointed out that she, too, appeared as a complex with which the ego-complex identified. In the case of our patient, it was not so much a negative figure, but rather a very infantile puella figure, a trophy wife, the beauty, who served only to impart an additional luster to the father's successes.

The patient's father also tried to mold her mother into the shape of this complex. This form of the anima is not capable of playing either a spiritually or an emotionally stimulating or leading role; rather, she remains an empty husk that serves only as a container for male projections. Of course, this sort of negative anima of the father can manifest in other shapes and guises. The male forms in which the feminine is devalued and declared inferior vary over the widest possible range. In *Männerphantasieno* (1977), Theweleit gives good examples of the split in these anima images, describing the patriarchal culture's division of the image of woman into the white, ideal, and moral figure (which, as our example demonstrates, is often empty) and the red, carnal, and demonic one. From the viewpoint of analytical psychology, however, we should guard against idealizing the "white woman" (or the "beautiful woman," another idealization) as a positive anima since, on the one hand, she can be an empty, egoless doll and, on the other, a cold witch.

Now we come to the second double pyramid. As in Jung's *Aion* (1959), I have situated the snake or serpent at the top pole. It is both the inferior pole of the shadow quaternio and the guardian over this third quaternio, which contains the animal and the vegetative precursors of the two higher quaternia. Referenced to the father complex, this quaternio takes the form sketched in figure 5.5:

FIGURE 5.5

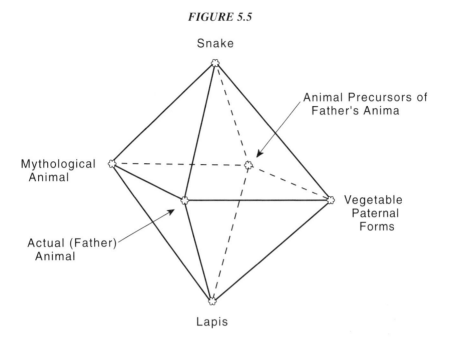

The snake is a great symbol that played a major role in alchemy as the Mercurius *non vulgi*. It symbolizes the primary *massa confusa* containing all the preoedipal, primary process activity in the unconscious realm of drives and instincts. The snake knows no moral categories, no human wishes, considerations, or compassionate warmth. Consequently, it can ignore all these human dimensions with complete lack of relatedness. But at the same time, it also has a close connection to the vegetative domain, since, as we know from the myth of paradise, it is a tree numen and is traditionally represented in a tree or even functioning as its trunk. As a dragon, it is the guardian of the treasure contained in this realm of drives and instincts. In the positive sense, with this double valence as serpent of salvation or (as in the Grimm tale of the "White Snake") as the voice of nature, it embodies many values that lie within this realm. This realm is far removed from consciousness and contains much that is capable of consciousness. But the serpent also appears to possess a unique and peculiar wisdom that is felt to be supernatural.

A word must be said about assigning the snake to the father archetype here and (as I will discuss later) to the mother archetype. Again and again, we forget that the animal world as well as the vegetable world has both sexes, and that we experience them in dream and fantasy as having both sexes. Consequently, we are all too facile in assigning the snake, for example, to the female, especially in the German language where it has a grammatically feminine gender, and because the times of Eve it has been associated with woman. Collective consciousness almost always directs the word *snake* as an insult to women. On the other hand, animals such as the lion or the eagle are almost always assigned to the masculine, although there are, of course, female lions and female eagles. I believe that this sort of discrimination can play a major role in dream interpretation. When symbols of this type appear, we should pay attention to whether they are masculine or feminine, and if need be, ask the patient. Of course, this is often difficult with certain animals. Who can tell a male snake from a female snake in a dream unless the dreamer is a zoologist? Nevertheless associations, both subjective and objective, that the patient brings to the symbol can clarify gender.

As an example, I would like to cite a male patient's dream in which both a male and a female snake appeared. At the time, this man was struggling with his sense of masculinity. He dreamt: "A small, very poisonous snake was in a room, and I observed how a second, bigger snake, approached the first one and began to swallow it. This filled me with a great sense of relief."

His associations to this dream, which I need not report in detail here, indicate that the small, poisonous snake was unequivocally associated to the dangerous, aggressive female elements, while he experienced the larger snake as a symbol of male strength, power, and dignity. Here this masculine principle was able to master the negative element of the feminine by incorporating it, to nurture itself with it and appropriate its aggressive capabilities in transmuted form, all of which began soon to show up in the patient's experience and behavior.

On the left side of the quaternio diagrammed above, in which the snake presides at the top, I have situated the animal forms assigned to the father archetype, dividing them into the mythological animal and the real paternal animal. While the mythological animal displays the characteristics of the mythologem, the real paternal animal are those forms that a child assigns to the father as a real animal, for example, "My father is as strong as an elephant." Here the symbolic meaning and scope are generally unconscious. Kos and Giermann (1973) offer a classic example of these sorts of real animal parents in their book, *Die verzauberte Familie*, in which we find both real and mythological animal images of parents; these animal figures have almost as much variety as the entire animal kingdom itself. But it is almost always a real animal in which the child sees certain qualities of the father personified, and that is why, in this context, I call it a "real" father animal or animal father.

In contrast to the personal animal which represents the father, we also have the mythological animal, which always has certain numinous qualities, as, for example, Poseidon's bull, entrusted to King Minos so that he could conquer Crete and secure his regency over a unified island. Those hybrid and fabulous animals that we know from the great variety of mythologies likewise belong in this category. Whether this sort of mythological animal should be assigned to the father or to the mother archetype can be decided by the sex of the animal or by the patient's associations and amplifications or by the material constellated in the analysis and by whether the patient's problem is more with the father or with the mother imago in the current phase of the analysis.

Next, on the right side of the pyramid, we have the animal representatives as precursors or pre-imagos of the father. Here I have forsworn differentiating between the mythological and the real. For all patients, these images refer to deeply unconscious material that usually arises only after a long analysis. To be able to deal with this, which is by no means always the case, the patient must differentiate between the masculine and feminine sides not only of the father but also of the father archetype. Hence, even when it first appears, this material contains a large proportion of collective imagos.

Last in this quaternio, as the fourth point, we reach an even deeper level that represents the vegetative realm of plants. The world of plants is not so strictly divided into masculine and feminine in our consciousness. Consequently, here too we must carefully discern from the analytic situation whether a given plant having a bisexual symbolism—a tree, for example— is to be assigned more to the domain of the father archetype or father complex, or to the mother in the specific patient's analytic situation. A typical example is a woman patient who felt herself to be entwined and suffocated in a dream where her father was a fir tree and her mother and sisters were flowering vines.

The bottom pole of this pyramid leads into inanimate nature. Again borrowing from Jung, I have taken as its leading exponent the lapis. It stands at the upper pole of this lowest and last pyramid, which I have left in the elementary realm with the same symbols that Jung has described and have made no alterations such as I did on the other pyramids. Figure 5.6 represents this pyramid.

I am proceeding on the premise that at this very deep level there is an extensive confluence of the mother and the father archetypes. Still, the lapis can be assigned to either the father or the mother archetype. The elements that are placed in this pyramid can also be experienced simultaneously as masculine or feminine. The fire of love is more feminine while the masculine form is closer to the thunderbolts hurled by Zeus. The same holds true for air, water, and earth. Not for nothing do most mythologies have both male and female deities for these four elements, and they can appear in the unconscious in these forms. However, I do make an important distinction in

FIGURE 5.6

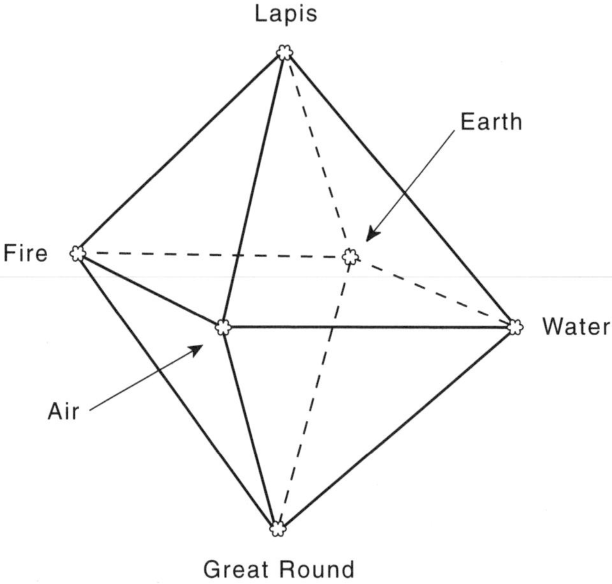

Lapis

Earth

Fire

Water

Air

Great Round

the lowest pole of the pyramid, the great round, where Jung makes no distinction: I assign the sun to the father archetype and the moon to the mother archetype. Thus, at the lowest poles in the cores of the great complexes, Sol and Luna face each other, as in the images of the *Rosarium* and in *The Psychology of the Transference* (Jung 1946/54b).

Since all male gods are associated with the sun and the female goddesses with the moon, these four pyramids can come together in a circular struc-

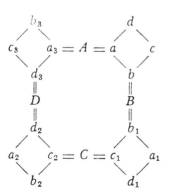

FIGURE 5.7 Summary of the four pyramids

ture in which the highest and the lowest join and are identical, as Jung has also described (see figure 5.7).

To bring this chapter to a close, I would like to present a dream from a much later stage in the treatment of the woman patient mentioned above. I have encountered the motif of this dream, with lesser or greater variations, in many analyses; I discuss another version in *Träume als Sprache der Seele* (Dieckmann 1972). Just as other dreams have done, this dream preceded or accompanied important and decisive changes in the life of this patient. In the first phase of her treatment, only father imagos were constellated and appeared in her dreams from within the upper two pyramids; then this dream revealed that the two lower pyramids had been mobilized and consequently effected significant processes of change.

> I am together with one of my older men friends in his apartment and am about to leave him. His appearance is vague. I leave his apartment and suddenly find myself in a dense forest that has a primeval quality to it. I feel very happy and have a deep connection with all nature around me. Suddenly, I am surprised to see a big snake coiled about a tree trunk. At first, I have the impulse to run away, but then I stop and look at the snake more closely. Gradually I am overtaken by a growing enthusiasm for the beauty of this snake. The longer I observe it, the more I like it and the more I get a feeling of relatedness with this animal. I can even understand its language, and it tells me that it is the King of the Snakes in this forest and might perhaps be able to help me. I awake from this dream with a deep feeling of happiness.

Following this dream, the patient seemed a good deal more grown up and less daughterly. Not long after, she became able to form relationships with men of her own age in which she experienced real feelings of pleasure in sexual activity and following which she was able to fall asleep relaxed.

This dream is reminiscent of *Beauty and the Beast* or of a Mediterranean tale of a snake in which a young woman's love and affection frees a prince from enchantment in a snake's body. Psychodynamically, this dream in the treatment of this patient corresponded to a phase in which she was able to open more affectionately to the world of her own drives and instincts, which she had previously experienced as frightening and shadowy. The core of the complex was expanded and, so to speak, opened downward. Through the snake in this dream, she found her first access to the wishes and needs of her own personality.

In addition to the snake, King of the Forest and of Nature and the central symbol in this dream, she could subsequently experience the vegetable realm of trees, bushes, and plants for the first time as filled with life. The little girl's love for her deified father spread to and cathected other realms, such as the earth on which she walked and the air she breathed, which was the breath of nature and not the pollution of the metropolis. I believe that this example beautifully illustrates how an essential individuation process was introduced through expanding and enriching the core of a complex that originally was restricted to four fixations.

CHAPTER 6

Diagnosing Positive and Negative Parental Complexes

Since I have already described in earlier chapters the form in which the elementary and the transformative characters of the parental complexes can be diagnosed, I will confine myself in this chapter to the diagnosis of the positive and the negative complexes. In order to establish more continuity with Jung's discussion, I will refer to the mother complex in discussing the problems of diagnosis.

It is striking how difficult it is not only for beginners but also for experienced analysts of the Jungian school to distinguish a negative mother complex from a positive one. The same holds true for the father complex. In part, this is due to the fact that the archetype, which forms the core of the complex, always has two poles and to the fact that the personal mother is never entirely white or black but, like every human being, a mixture of positive and negative characteristics. In practice we do, of course, often find these two poles dissociated. The majority of our patients, and probably the majority of people in general, tend to regard their mothers as either good or bad. When they do this, the opposite pole is repressed into the unconscious, and the individual can no longer experience it adequately. In the case of a patient for whom love, affection, respect, honor, and relatedness to the mother occupies the foreground, this means that disappointment, aversion, even hate, envy, aggression, and often justified criticism of the mother are repressed. We would be fully justified in saying that, in the eyes of the child, mothers, and of course fathers, too, are seldom complete human beings with all their ambivalences considered but rather, as a rule, are carriers of the projected archetype of the Great Mother or the Great Father. These projections often prove to be so tenacious that an entire lifetime is barely, or only rarely, long enough to withdraw or work them through.

Moreover, and this is the second diagnostic difficulty that repeatedly causes confusion, Jung himself never precisely or clearly defined what he meant by "positive" and "negative" mother complexes. As a rule, he always writes very generally about the mother or the father complex. There are only a few passages in his works from which we can ascertain that he is basing a positive or negative diagnosis on the more conscious part of the complex. Here I refer particularly to his essay, "Psychological Aspects of the Mother Archetype" (1954/59). In this essay, he speaks very clearly of the positive and negative effects of the mother complex on the daughter, such that we can assume that by the term *positive mother complex* he means that part of the complex that influences the conscious ego and its experience and behavior. This part of the complex can operate in a fully or partially conscious manner or largely unconsciously. The negative pole—containing the intense jealousy of the mother, the incestuous bond with the father, and the attempt to trump the mother—often remains deeply repressed. Later, in the same essay, Jung clearly expresses his view: as the perfect example, he describes the negative mother complex of a daughter who does not want to be like her mother at any price.

In the following discussion, I will hold to this form of diagnosis and consequently designate a positive mother complex as one in which the subject, be it man or woman, experiences the mother predominantly as loving, good, and positive with the negative feelings toward the mother by and large deeply repressed. The reverse holds true for the negative mother complex, and of course both designations also apply to the father complex.

A further problem in diagnosis arises in that some authors (Kast (1980), for example) understand a positive complex to be healthy, ranking it among those that form the complex structure of the normal psyche. Later in the same book, which deals with the association experiment in clinical practice, Kast describes an obviously positive father complex; however, she does not label it positive but instead dominating and negative. This conception is not without justification; Jung himself in his essay on the mother complex of the daughter describes the positive sides of the complex as healthy character traits and sees only their exaggeration as negative and pathological. However, Kast also says of the positive complex that it "does not have to be conflictual," and by saying this she includes the possibility that positive complexes can cause conflicts.

I must now discuss why I use the designations "positive" and "negative" in diagnosis, since they are obviously problematic, rather than, say, "conscious" and "unconscious," "dominant" and "split off," or a similar opposition. This confronts us with some important diagnostic considerations and aids. Jung found it important to speak of the "feeling-toned complex." This means that the decisive accent is placed on the feeling tone and not on the words or on the spoken content that the patient presents. However, when speaking of feelings, we distinguish between groups of positive and negative feeling tones brought to bear on another person, thing, or ourselves. There is no cause to diverge from this usage here.

Recognizing the feeling tone independent of the lexical content sometimes presents difficulties, specifically where a patient, for example, praises and acknowledges the mother while one senses negative criticism and rejection behind the words. Shakespeare offered a classic example in *Julius Caesar* in Brutus's funeral oration where we hear Anthony repeat "but Brutus was an honorable man!" again and again. Often it takes the analyst's schooled empathy to detect such undertones in a speech praising the mother, since the dear little mother of the elementary school primer is still a sacred image for many. The same holds true for the opposite situation: not infrequently at the beginning of an analysis, the patient devalues or criticizes the mother, while behind the words the analyst senses a deep love. A twenty-five-year-old male patient offered a good example of this.

> At first, he spoke in derogatory terms about his dyed-in-the-wool conservative "old folks." But through his words one noticed that this sounded very contrived, and he soon developed a strong positive mother transference to the female analyst to whom I had referred him. It further came to light that he had undertaken the study of theology because it had been his mother's ardent wish to see her son in the pulpit. He also identified with his mother to the extent that he had sought a part-time job as a nursing assistant, devotedly caring for frail old people. Contrary to appearances, the negative feeling tone of the complex—one could say the "negative mother complex"—was deeply repressed and found expression only in his symptoms, as is typically the rule with the repressed, opposite pole of a complex. He had a whole series of witch dreams that came to the surface after being in analysis for period of time, and tormenting feelings of hate for the persons he was taking care of attacked him, all of which was initially concealed under a mantle of depression and disruptions in his work.

In chapter 4 I gave an example of a negative mother complex that could be only indirectly accessed. In that case, the patient's mother had died when he was twelve, and he had repressed all memories of her. This sort of lacuna is, of course, always suspect in regard to something negative and disappointing. However, it can also occur in the instance of a positive complex when the intent is to avoid awakening the deep pain around an inadequately resolved loss of a loved one. In the case of the patient in chapter 4, repressing memories of his mother permitted only the indirect inference of a negative mother complex which found expression in wild hate for his mother-in-law and the deep anxieties he had about his wife. At the same time, it was characteristic of the presence of a negative mother complex projected not only onto his mother-in-law but also onto his wife that, shortly following the marriage, conflict between the spouses broke out and his symptoms became considerably worse. One soon noticed from the manner in which he spoke of his wife that he actually rejected her and under the surface even hated her, although he displaced all his hate to his evil mother-in-law.

An additional diagnostic problem arises when a patient presents a balanced ambivalence toward both parental figures. Then it is often difficult to decide which pole of the archetype informs the dominant complex core. In these cases, one should not hesitate to leave the diagnosis tentative, waiting to see which complex is constellated in the analysis and which complex one can more meaningfully work on at a given time.

Here, it is important to repeat the obvious: every human being and hence every patient has both mother and father complexes. In the course of an analysis, both have to be worked on, made conscious, and worked through in all their subtleties to the extent possible. It never happens that only one is present without the other, neither the mother complex without the father complex, nor the negative pole without the positive. But it is characteristic of all neuroses that at a given moment one specific complex predominates and is dissociated from the other complexes. Naturally, this tends to change in the course of an analysis. The more fully and comprehensively the initially dominant complex is worked through, the more other complexes appear behind it. In my opinion, we can speak of a successful analysis, as I will demonstrate later in my discussion of a borderline case, when at the end of treatment the patient emerges from the monotony of a dominant complex and the psyche again has access to a network of various complexes in relationship to one another.

The significance of diagnosis in therapeutic treatment and whether or not it makes sense to diagnose remains open for discussion. There are analysts who hold the view that diagnosis as well as anamnesis is better *not* done at the beginning of analytic therapy but rather at the end. In my view, however, a diagnosis of the complexes is thoroughly worthwhile at the beginning of treatment and should be repeated again and again in the course of therapy. Therapeutic endeavors can then be guided by our diagnoses. This would be simple if we could say, for example, that when there is a negative mother complex with elementary character the appropriate therapeutic intervention would be to emphasize in our interpretations the complex cores of the positive pole of the mother archetype with transformative character. Then it would make sense, if this were the case, to work toward a triangulation, where the mobilization of a positive father complex offered protection against the negative mother.

Unfortunately the analytic process is not so rational and obvious an undertaking. In one or another case, what has just been described might be absolutely correct. But more often it is the case that the dominant, constellated complex is not fully conscious but rather, at best, only partially so or even completely unconscious (as I described above in the instance of the theology student). Hence, as a rule, in the first phase of analysis we must work for a long time on this dominant complex in order to make it conscious in all its shades of feeling tone. As discussed in chapter 4, it does not suffice that, at the end of treatment, the patient is again conscious of his negative experience of mother; rather, healing this patient's severe symptoms demonstrates how important it was to get to the archetypal cores of the negative mother complex in the figures of the witch and the *Höllandermichel*. Nor is it enough only to make the patient aware of these figures; they must enter the transference-countertransference constellation so that they can be worked on there.

In every treatment, new and different problems and ways of dealing with the constellated complex arise, and the best assistants available to the analyst are always the patient's dreams and fantasies and the contents and feelings constellated in the transference. And we must not forget the analyst's dreams of the patient as well as his or her countertransference reactions. But the prerequisite for being able to deal empathically with the complex is to have recognized it. We can then avoid taking projections all too personally. We can better understand them and meet them with the necessary objectivity.

This brings us to one final fact that always plays a major role in psychotherapeutic and psychoanalytic diagnosis, and which I have discussed elsewhere in greater detail (Dieckmann 1991). I am referring to the influence of the transference situation on diagnosis. Control analysts and teachers with many years' experience have found that the second time one meets a patient who has had a first interview or an anamnesis with a candidate-in-training, a different complex from the one diagnosed in the first interview is constellated thanks to the influence of the personality of a different analyst. Many external aspects also play a role, for example, age differences, change from a female analyst to a male analyst, differing analytic settings or furnishings of the consultation room, and the like. But certainly the more significant influences operating in the background are the different personality and character structures as well as the differing typologies of the two participating analysts. Depending on these differences, different complexes can be constellated in the two interviews in so far as the patient's dominant complex is not rigidly fixated and the ego largely cathected by it (which tends to be the exception). Consequently, it is difficult to say that the candidate has made a diagnostic error if he or she arrives at a different view than the training analyst. Unfortunately, or perhaps fortunately, our discipline bursts the bounds of objectivity: as Pauli (1955) has said of physics, the observed object is directly dependent on the observing subject. We could also say with Heisenberg that in modern psychology just as in modern physics there is a kind of "uncertainty principle" that permits no fixed results. But this does not play a detrimental role in the therapeutic situation; rather, it can be an additional support for the practitioner who is thereby alerted to the presence of other complex cores. In analysis, the therapist must let the patient take the lead and must deal with the complex that is constellated at each point in the treatment.

In discussing this chapter with colleagues after presenting it at the C. G. Jung Institute of Berlin, H. J. Wilke made some observations on the scientific understanding of the formation of complexes. He stated:

> The classical division into simple and complex in science applied to the domains of physics and the biological sciences. Physics is simple and predictable in the realm of mechanics, and accessible to anyone. The mathematics of calculating the position of an undiscovered planet may be complicated, but its calculability proves its simplicity as an unambiguous determinism. All life processes are complex, that is, manifold and unpredictable. In contrast to physical determinism, all living things have degrees of freedom that can confound all calculations and predictions, and, at a minimum, relativize them. The future behavior of the AIDS virus is as little predictable as is the economy or the social behavior of the individual or the human group.
>
> This boundary between the simple and the complex is shifting significantly in contemporary science and appears almost to be dissolving. When energy is produced, perhaps at various levels, simple physical processes create structures and develop stable states which can rhythmically oscillate with precision and regularity among these levels. A simple example of these sorts of complex organizing structures occurs in the convection flows in heating water in the so-called Bénard cells. Approximately 10^{21} water molecules form one such cell and rotate alternately one to the right and one to the left. The direction of rotation and the order of the cells cannot be calculated beforehand. Another noteworthy example is the proof of chemical combinations in the cosmos that form part of the fundamental building blocks of life along with the polymolecular carbon ring structures that do not occur on Earth under normal conditions.
>
> This fundamentally revises our understanding of physical nature. The law of entropy is relativized, and taking this as a starting point we infer that there is in physical nature, in addition to entropy, a tendency toward forming stable, nonhomeostatic conditions. Hence the origin of life as a supremely complex and extremely nonhomeostatic condition can no longer be counted among chance occurrences but rather must be understood as a process inherent in the nature of matter and energy. In our contemporary understanding of science, an extremely wide arc is taking

shape that links the complexities and indeterminacies of the processes ranging from the origin of the cosmos, to the origin of life, to the social processes and intellectual developments and currents in an evolutionary paradigm. In the framework of this sort of evolutionary hypothesis, even Jung's theory of the complexes, the notion of homeostatic neurotic conditions, and the various stabilities in neuroses, as well as the binding of energy in such psychic structures, finds room and no longer needs to stand more in opposition to the methods and working hypotheses of modern research in the natural sciences.

Finally, we need to mention briefly that we can diagnose complexes by means of Jung's word association experiment, which Meier (1968) values and Kast (1980) describes in detail. Beebe, too, has dealt in detail with the relationship of the various complexes and type functions. Here I would mention only Beebe's brief comment on Eckström's paper (Beebe 1988). According to Beebe, the leading function is typically characterized by the archetypal figure of the hero. The inferior function, on the other hand, is carried by the contrasexual archetype, the anima in the man and the animus in the woman. The auxiliary function is oriented toward the father in the male and toward the mother in the female. The second auxiliary, standing closest to the inferior function, has qualities of the puer aeternus in the man and of the puella aeterna in the woman. Beebe is of the opinion that these four complexes swing back and forth between extraversion and introversion, and that people who can experience all four of these functions can experience a condition of wholeness, or at least a taste of it.

Simultaneously, Beebe establishes next to this structure the four shadow functions with their opposed extraverted and introverted behavior. These four shadow complexes are much more difficult to experience as part of one's personality. They are either projected or function completely independently of consciousness. They correspond to the daemonic personality: to the negative senex or trickster in the man and to the negative mother in the woman. It is to be hoped that, in combination with Jung's very intuitive observations on the pathology of the types which nevertheless is often found to be surprisingly apt, from the work Jung's followers and from Beebe's very interesting ideas, we can someday develop a more specialized doctrine of the neuroses. But that is not our focus here.

CHAPTER 7

The Pathology of the Positive Mother Complex

Since negative mother complexes and both positive and negative father complexes have been discussed in other chapters, I would like to present an example of the pathology of a positive mother complex in greater detail here.

In his oft cited essay on the mother complex, Jung (1954/59) indirectly gave definitions the positive and the negative mother complexes. I want to repeat that in a positive mother complex he is referring to a far-reaching identification with the mother or with the archetypal maternal in its several variations. As we can see when we look through Jung's opus, this definition applies equally to his description of the mother complex in the son. Both in the initial interview and in the early stages of therapy, it is relatively easy in a great number of cases to discern whether this leitmotiv evokes a beneficial, beguiling, pleasant, happy, and endearing melody or feelings in the listener, or whether quite the opposite appears in disharmonies, anger, rage, vexation, or rejection. Cast in our terminology, we would say that the complex in question is powered with either positive libido or aggressive emotions.

This diagnosis suggests itself since a complex is typically characterized and usually very noticeable by its particular feeling tone. Jung himself compared it with the leitmotivs of Wagnerian music that are always heard when an important figure makes an appearance. A mother complex leitmotiv is always relatively easy to recognize when a patient starts to speak of his or her mother. Only infrequently will a patient speak of his or her mother as an average human being with her faults and weaknesses as well as her strengths and virtues at the beginning of therapy. An archetypal motif always echoes through the words that are pronounced over the mother, with the sense of either an idealization or a demonization. The more distinctly the complex is developed and the stronger its dominance in the psyche, the more one-sided and noticeable the motif tends to be. Since the complex as such does not signify anything pathological, of course, we find this phenomenon also among people who are not patients.

The painter Marc Chagall offers a particularly beautiful and clear example of a strongly positive mother complex in his autobiography where he describes his mother in the following words:

> Mother sat in front of the great stove, one hand on the table, the other across her lap. Her head held rigidly erect under her hair bun crowned with a needle. She rapped her finger on the table, several times, and then said, "Everybody's asleep. What sort of children do I have? Isn't there anybody who will chat with me?" She loved to chat. . . . But she had nobody. I alone heard her from a distance. She called to me, "My son, come talk with me!" But I am only a street urchin, and my mother a queen. What am I supposed to talk about with her? (1960)

It is clear how positively, lovingly, and respectfully Chagall as an adult recounts his memories of his mother. In another passage in his autobiography, he says of her, "When I try to speak of her, sometimes I cannot talk but have to sob."

Quite the opposite is the case with the poet Rainer Maria Rilke. Here we find a very distinct negative mother complex in which he completely rejects personal mother. His leitmotiv is "Be anything, just not like Mother!" On April 15, 1904, Rilke wrote to Lou:

> Mother came to Rome. Every meeting with her is a sort of relapse. Whenever I have to look at this unreal, lost woman who has no connections with anything and who cannot age, I feel how already as a child I struggled to get away from her, and I fear that after years of running I am still not far enough away from her, that inside somewhere I still have movements that are the other half of her impoverished gestures. . . ; then I dread her absentminded piety, her obstinate belief, all these distortions and deceptions she hangs on to, and she herself, empty as a dress, spectral and horrible, and that I am still her child; that somewhere in this blank wall attached to nothing was a scarcely recognizable trap door that was my portal to the world. (Quoted in Dieckmann 1981a)

An early verse he wrote testifies to the same attitude:

> But my Mother came
> to give them flowers.
> My mother took
> the flowers from my life.

Of course, we do not often find the distinction between a positive and a negative mother complex in our patients expressed as clearly as the poet and the painter do. There are some extreme cases in which the idealization or demonization is very clear. Between these two extremes, we find all the gradations and intermediate steps in the individual case where it is certainly not always easy to decide whether a more positive or a more negative mother complex is present. But usually we succeed in the first interview, or if there are still doubts, they tend to clarified in the early sessions.

On the hypothesis of the compensatory function of the unconscious, we would expect that when a positive mother complex is known to or well established in consciousness the negative aspect would appear in the unconscious. Here the imago of even the personal mother would have to appear in a negative, coldly rejecting, frustrating, wounding, morally inferior, or similar form. This is very seldom the case in actual therapy, and in spite of an intensive search, I have not found one patient from my practice over the years whom I could present as an example. This phenomenon seems to me to be characteristic of the positive mother complex. In contrast to this, I could offer a few examples of the negative mother complex. And of course, this cannot be a scientifically "objective" statement, but rather must be taken with a grain of salt, since we must always take into account the transference and our countertransference.

In the diagnosis and therapy of the complexes, the relationship between consciousness and the unconscious appears to be somewhat more complex than a simple principle of compensation would lead us to believe. Complexes, even when they are known to consciousness, reach deep into the unconscious and beyond, into the collective unconscious. The more powerfully energized a complex, and the more it dominates the psyche in pathological form, the more associations and amplifications it draws to itself in the unconscious and the more these associations and amplifications must remain unconscious. Through these central images of the complexes we arrive at a kind of landscape of the soul with all its seams, connections, branches, transitions, and border areas. The advantage of imaging the complexes lies in the possibility of visualizing the countless individual positions occupied by the variety and multiplicity of neurotic and normal experience as well as the general characteristics of the complex. But the essential factors shaping this landscape of the soul are the energy dynamics and structure of the complexes and the archetypes that underlie them. Thereby a relationship is established between concrete image and our theory.

I have described a similar phenomenon in a number of essays on the dream ego (Dieckmann 1965, 1977a, 1978a, 1985). The dream ego never thinks of assuming a different mode of experiencing and behaving than the conscious ego. Only when changes and transformations emerge in the analytic process do the dream ego's modes of experiencing and behaving begin to change. Something similar seems to be the case with pathologically overdetermined complexes. Due to their ramifications in the unconscious and their roots in the archetypal core of the complex, dreams and fantasies always produce positive images of the mother extending into the realm of the collective unconscious long into the first phase of analytic therapy when there is a positive mother complex. As I have illustrated with two clinical examples in my treatment of borderline symbolism, the libidinal charge of a specific complex core at the archetypal level is so high that for a long time nothing else can emerge (Dieckmann 1988). Superficially, one might say that a patient with a positive mother complex doesn't dare to dream that Mother also has negative and destructive sides.

Here I would like to share one more, very beautiful example from Chagall that clearly shows in one image the depths and dimensions to which the mother imago possessed by a positive complex can dominate a person's psyche.

In 1917, Chagall painted a well-known portrait of his first wife; it is called "Bella with the White Collar." His wife was the daughter of a rich jeweler from Vitebsk, from a higher social stratum than Chagall, the son of a simple laborer in a herring factory. He had married her in 1914 under conditions equally difficult as those of the courtship. A female figure, a Demeter/grain goddess who bends over the world as a giant deity, dominates the entire painting. In the foreground stand two minute figures representing Chagall himself and his little daughter, Ida. The archetypal projection of the dominant and powerful mother imago has migrated to his young wife. As a rule, it is true that the unconscious image of the mother is projected onto the fiancee or wife, and the intensity of the projection most certainly depends on the degree to which the positive mother complex was still dominant and powerful at the time. The real Mother Chagall was a very small woman and often compared with a female Napoleon. It would have been closer to reality to paint small, vital figures, especially since Bella was not large but rather dainty (Dieckmann 1981c).

While the portrait bears the personal features of Bella Chagall, it is nevertheless apparent that what we have here is a grain goddess to whom mortal humans are only tiny, insignificant creatures. But this sort of fertility goddess also carries a thoroughly positive and prospective significance when she is constellated in the unconscious of a creative person. She symbolizes not only the regressive longing to return to the womb of the Great Mother, but also the creative potential of a person of genius. One might say that Chagall's opus corresponds to this gigantic Demeter who permits the small human being to grow beyond himself. We are involuntarily reminded of Goethe's equally positive mother complex and his verses from *Dichtung und Wahrheit* (*Poetry and Truth*):

Vom Vater hab ich die Statur
des Lebens ernstes Führen,
vom Mütterchen die Frohnatur
die Lust zu fabulieren.*

Having defined and described the positive mother complex, I do not want to limit my observations to the prospective aspect. Its pathology prevents our patients from living their own lives and keeps them enclosed in this complex or, as I will discuss below, derails them by its influence. This corresponds to two differing forms in which the positive mother complex can find expression in a patient. In one form, it can constrict, impede, and suffocate the initiative, activity, expansiveness, and development of the ego-complex and of self-actualization; in the second form, it can narcissistically exaggerate, inflate, and seduce the patient's ego-complex and self-actualization into activities that are ultimately destructive. Two characteristic images of the mother introject stand behind these two forms; we can designate one as constrictive and the other as seductive. They correspond to the two fundamental characters of the Great Feminine that Neumann (1955) designated as elementary and transformative. We can illustrate this with two typical clinical examples.

Peter was a small, slightly built social worker who entered analysis because of his bronchial asthma. It had begun when his wife separated from him after five years of marriage at the same time that his mother died. His mother had been a housewife, and he had idealized her and characterized her as very loving, overly caring, warm-hearted, self-sacrificing, but also anxious and passive without much initiative of her own. He led a constricted life. Although well liked by his colleagues, he had little success in his profession because he was unable to set boundaries against excessive demands from people seeking his help. In his private life, he had few interests. As a couple, he and his wife had not had a circle of friends but only a few fleeting acquaintances. For his part, he preferred to sit at home in his free time, reading newspapers and magazines or watching television. The few activities he and his wife had undertaken were on her initiative. It was also characteristic of him that he had scarcely any dreams until long after the beginning of analysis, and his access to his inner world and fantasy life was difficult.

Helmuth, in comparison, was a forty-six-year-old, thoroughly active and successful merchant. After completing a degree in business, he had

---

*Father gave me character / to lead a serious life, / from Mother I got a happy nature / and joy in spinning tales.

joined a large firm, was soon launched on his career, and managed a large division that demanded much travel. He sought analysis because of increasingly depressive moods, arhythmia, and feelings of emptiness and meaninglessness. When he was eight, his parents' violently conflictual marriage had failed, and his father had left the family. Helmuth, who had a younger brother, was his mother's favorite. Theirs was an intimate relationship, and in her fantasies his mother expected great and special things of him, of which in part she told him. He described her as an active, lively woman, full of ideas and imaginative. She had a small stationery shop and continually had unusual ideas for enlarging it. Unfortunately, most of her attempts misfired, and except for a small, adjacent lending library, which for my book-loving patient was of great importance, all her attempts ended in bankruptcy. The family lived in constant debt and obligations, combined with fear of the collapse of their livelihood.

Helmuth, however, had success in his career and fulfilled many of his mother's expectations. He was a typical manager with great powers of persuasion who got along very well with his business partners. He, too, had a lively fantasy life, and frequently he had new and profitable ideas. He was also restless in his domestic life. He had a wife and three children, and had an active social life with a large circle of friends. In addition, he was interested in music and theater and attended at least one performance each week when his business travel permitted. Fleeting liaisons with other women were also the rule with him. In contrast to Peter, Helmuth offered me a number of quite colorful and interesting dreams from the very beginning of analysis. It was characteristic of them that for a long time the figure of his mother was absent, although in his associations he said a lot about her. When she did finally make an appearance in the dreams, she was initially a positive or neutral figure.

These examples clearly show that the first patient, Peter, had a positive mother complex with elementary character. The negative consequences of a mother complex with elementary character, as Neumann has described them, can be seen clearly in Peter's personality and way of life. Peter's expansivity was suffocated and completely restricted by the care-giving and protective element of the mother imago. In a certain sense, he was still contained in a maternal womb, which he experienced as positive and which he had hoped to find again in his wife. Likewise, in his profession, he had looked for a protective, care-giving, and thus pacifying activity which offered the element of a positive, protective space. Viewed symbolically, his home was the warm, maternal body cavity into which he could retreat from all the perils and disappointments of life. Almost nothing penetrated this from outside. There he felt completely comfortable; he fell ill only when his wife could no longer tolerate such a restricted life and broke free.

By contrast, Helmuth's inner image of his mother mobilized the transformative character of the Magna Mater at the archetypal level. The seductive mother caused him to seek further narcissistic confirmation in a hectic, active, and expansive life. His talent and diligence brought him the corresponding successes with which another person would have been satisfied and proud. But again and again he experienced himself as a failure, just as his mother had been with her plans. Ultimately, nothing could fulfill the demand of his excessively high ideals, and so, on the go and always changing, he restlessly chased from one task to another and, in his relationships, from one woman to the next. We cannot call his womanizing Don Juanism, as Jung (1954/59) does in his essay on the man's mother complex. Gradually his relationships, like his professional undertakings, lost their meaning and vitality. He was no longer satisfied by the excessive demands he put on himself and, thus in perpetual motion, had to move on to the next object. His illness began at the threshold of midlife when he began to sense that his path could not forever continue upwards and that professionally and in his family only a few modifications were still possible since, externally, he had in fact achieved everything possible. His illness did not come on suddenly, as was Peter's case, but rather crept up on him gradually over a period of several years.

Now I want to explore the archetypal figures that form the core of these two patients' complexes. We have already met this figure in Chagall's painting. The archetype of the Magna Mater, the Great Mother, who shone through in the fantasies and dreams, partly in symbolic and partly in direct form, was a goddess of grain and of fertility, primarily of a nurturing character at the oral level. This corresponds to Demeter in Greek mythology, and to Ceres in Roman mythology, who is largely identical with Demeter. Thanks to the Greeks' magnificent intuition regarding this complex phenomenon, it is characteristic of this goddess that she is always depicted in two forms. Demeter is always accompanied by her daughter, Kore, who becomes Persephone, coruler of the underworld, after being abducted by and married to Hades. For one-third of the year she descends into the underworld realm, and for the remaining two-thirds returns to the surface of the earth, there to live with her mother as Kore. Roman mythology adopted this abduction of Ceres's daughter Liberia by Pluto and her ascent and descent practically unaltered (Roscher 1978).

In Greek art, daughter and mother are depicted in such away that they are practically indistinguishable in most representations which show them together. Both Demeter and Persephone are characterized as goddesses of grain in antique art by wreaths and blades of grain that they carry in their hands. According to myth, it is Demeter who first revealed the secret of

*FIGURE 7.1 Demeter, Triptolemus,
and Persephone*

grain to the Athenians. They taught this discovery to Triptolemus and had him disseminate it as a sort of itinerant preacher (Sauerland 1941) (figure 7.1).

Here one can clearly see the virtual identity of mother and daughter. Between them stands the figure of Triptolemus, Prince of Eleusis, as a small human figure between the two powerful and great goddesses.

Frazer (1913) disagrees with the idea that the two goddesses were mythical embodiments of two different aspects as easy to distinguish as the earth and the vegetation that proceeds from it. He proposes that mother and daughter personify the grain in its double form, once as the ripe grain of the current year and the other as the seed corn of the coming year that descends into the earth in order to rise again as new growth. Precursors of this double, highly developed goddess, to whom magnificent temples were erected, are the worldwide folk customs pertaining to the Grain Mother and Grain Daughter, of which Frazer has collected numerous and convincing examples. In this sense, Demeter would always be the old spirit of the grain and Kore/Persephone the young or new spirit.

If we now transfer Frazer's hypotheses to the intrapsychic level relevant to our discussion, we find in very convincing form the personification of the fundamental character of the Great Feminine that Neumann has described. Demeter corresponds to the preserving, containing, and care-giving elementary character, while Kore/Persephone is an ever-changing figure, descending into the earth (Hades) and being transformed from the seed to the sprout and ultimately into the mature grain. Hence she becomes the image of eternal self-transformation, the transformative character of the Great Mother.

Both goddesses have positive, productive, and beneficent aspects as well as destructive and devastating ones. Basically, Demeter was a gentle nature, but she could be malicious (Ranke-Graves 1960). She damned Erysichthon, who had dared fell trees in her sacred grove, to eternal hunger. Regardless what he ate, his ravenous hunger could not be stilled, and he had to go begging on the streets for table scraps. She cast Askalaphos, the traitor, into a pit that she sealed with a gigantic boulder, and after Heracles had freed him, she turned him into an owl. She also refused to provide mankind with the fruits of the earth after Hades had abducted her daughter. The entire earth became waste, the soil desiccated and parched, in which no seed would sprout. Even the plain of Raris at Eleusis lay barren and fallow where usually fields of golden grain waved.

The name Persephone itself hints at something destructive (Roscher 1978). It derives from *phero* or *phonos*, she who causes destruction. In Rome, she was also called Proserpina, the fearsome. Originally, it seems, this was the name of a nymph sacrificed to the sacred year king. As we know from the *Odyssey*, in the underworld she (as did Athene) commanded the head of Medusa, which she sent to meet those who trespassed into Hades. They were turned to stone at the sight of it.

We can apply these dark aspects of the elementary and transformative character to our two patients and again encounter their symptoms. For Peter, the world had become a wasteland in which nothing could grow and where there was not even enough air to breathe. In contrast, Helmuth was paralyzed in his depression, and the narcissistic splendor of his accomplishments was slain by his illness. Even if the positive mother complex in both appeared to cathect the entire psychic realm, we yet find the negative mother archetype in symbolism and symptoms.

Once again, this raises the question as to the compensatory function of the unconscious and to the images and symbols of the negative mother. Here they appear to be completely overgrown and obscured by the complex. Peter split off the dark, evil, negative feminine in the form of porno-graphic fantasies and his collection of magazines, which he secretly accu-mulated at home while his marriage was still intact. As Theweleit (1977) has described, he had split the good, white woman from the evil, lowly, red woman. Helmuth's case was not as clear. As I have already described, it was characteristic of him that women emptied him emotionally. Even at the beginning of his analysis, dreams contained many feminine symbols distin-guished by this emptiness, for example, empty suitcases, briefcases from which the contents had been stolen, or an empty egg shell. Despite his many dreams, however, there was never a distinctly negative or threatening mother or anima figure to be found during the first phase of his analysis. To the extent that women appeared, they were either friendly toward him or neutral. Then he had a dream that greatly impressed him in which he met a powerful queen who graciously protected him. In working on this dream, it became clear to him which archetypal background figure he had experi-enced in his mother and he realized that he continued to project this figure onto the women around him. Only following this dream did negative fe-male figures appear, and his early idealization of his mother began to dis-solve. He was then able to have it out with the negative, witchy aspects of the seductive feminine.

I have described this dynamic in another case vignette of a negative mother complex (Dieckmann 1987b). First the archetypal background of the dynamics of the complex had to become clear and conscious before the other side, that is, the negative mother in the case of a positive mother com-plex, could appear at all. Certainly this does not always have to be the case. In my experience, however, the more one-sided the complex with its ideal-izations of the positive and its demonizations of the negative, the more likely this will arise. The stronger these idealizations and demonizations are, the more powerfully the opposite pole is repressed into the uncon-scious, and we access it only by way of making conscious the archetypal roots.

In this chapter, I have been concerned with making the reader aware that in diagnosing complexes it is not enough simply to diagnose a certain com-plex, but rather that we must differentiate them. Diagnosis of a mother complex says very little unless we know whether it is positive or negative and whether is determined more by the elementary or by the transformative character of the feminine. Of course, the same holds true for the father complex, where the archetypal figures of the father can tend more toward an Apollonian severity and rigidity or a Dionysian, intoxicating, and deduc-tive experience. Likewise, it is also necessary in the therapeutic process to direct one's attention again and again to the specific psychic complex. We should strive to make the complex conscious right down to its archetypal roots. Concurrently or subsequently, it is important to activate other, compensatory complex cores of the great parental imagos in order to reestablish a healthier and more normal complex structure in the psyche. Only when this succeeds can the symptoms yield to other possible modes of experiencing. We experience the other person as a real person only when we can withdraw the archetypal projections and neither demonize nor idealize him or her.

CHAPTER 8

The Formation of and Dealing with Symbols in the Complex Core, Exemplified in Two Borderline Cases

From the beginning of my analytic work, I have been especially interested in and touched by the highly charged emotional symbols that emerge from the unconscious of borderline and psychotic patients. In this chapter, I do not want to give a purely theoretical presentation but rather underline and clarify my reflections with more extensive clinical examples. But before describing those cases, I would like to present the main hypotheses on which I base my reflections.

1. In my experience with patients who show early disturbance—whether borderline patients or those with psychoses—we often find many archetypal symbols at the beginning of therapy. Jung (1952) described this experience and utilized it as a diagnostic criterion.

2. Jacobi (1959) states that, as long as it is archetypal, the symbol is an image presented to consciousness; or, as I would prefer to say, the image presented to consciousness represents the process of the archetypal structure per se, which is determined in part by the cultural context and in part by the individual's personal life experience. I would like to call attention to William's conclusion that the personal and the collective unconscious are

---

This chapter originally appeared in a different form in Stein and Schwartz-Salant, *The Borderline Personality in Analysis* (Wilmette: Chiron Publications, 1988). Tr.

indivisible: "Nothing in the personal experience needs to be repressed unless the ego feels threatened by its archetypal power" and "the archetypal activity which forms the individual myth is dependent on the material supplied by the personal unconscious" (William 1963). Both points underscore my thesis.

3. Provided we start by assuming a differentiated part of the complex personified in the archetypal symbols of the two great, fundamental complexes—the mother complex and the father complex—the archetypal symbol presented to consciousness corresponds to the center of a part of the core of the complex.[1] To a great extent we can, in my opinion, derive all the other complexes from these two basic complexes.

4. This complex core dominates both psyche and a more or less unstable ego and leads, as Whitmont (1969) described, to the fundamental mechanisms of projection and identity. *Identity* is to be distinguished from *identification* since identity is a completely unconscious condition that reaches much deeper. Reduced to a simple formula, we can say that the patient is unconsciously at the mercy of the constellated complex, corresponding to parts of the father or mother complex inclusive of their archetypal and collective components. I would like to emphasize that this does not exclude the other defense mechanisms, such as active splitting (Kernberg 1975) and projective identification (Klein 1946), which are characteristic of these patients.

5. While I was still closely following Jung's conception (a similar one can be found in Freud, by the way) in my book of fairy tales and symbols (Dieckmann 1977b) that the dream symbol was a vehicle of meaning that arose spontaneously from the unconscious, in recent years I have come to have doubts about this based on my practical analytic work. I still agree with Jung that the symbol makes it possible to visualize contents which could not be represented in another or better manner than through such an image. It translates the abstract world of instincts into a vivid image and makes it a psychic event which provides the instinct with meaning and direction. I think, however, that there are symbols that undergo development and that—as Kreitler (1965) describes for the conscious creation of symbols—there are creative processes in the unconscious that have a development long before they emerge into consciousness. In the further course of analysis, symbols continue to be worked through in a partially conscious, partially unconscious, manner in which, I believe, thinking, feeling, sensing, and intuitive processes play a role. I differ in this regard from Kreitler's experimental examination in which she assumed only the rational processes of thinking were involved in symbol formation.

---

[1]Erich Neumann discussed this in detail in *The Great Mother* (1955).

Therefore I suggest not speaking of the symbol "arising spontaneously" as a vehicle of meaning but rather as one spontaneously "appearing" in consciousness. In my first case vignette, I will try to illustrate this with an example in which I trace the first attempts to form a central archetypal symbol in the initial dream back to the personal history of childhood.

6. I proceed on the assumption that, in the specific analytic situation, transference and countertransference play an important role in the formation of symbols. We could not otherwise explain how patients who change analysts, especially when they change from analysts of one school to another, often react with considerable alteration in their dream symbols. Differentiated patients in particular often mention this difference with astonishment. Leaving aside the hypothesis of obliging dreams, which seems to me quite shallow, I can imagine that the unconscious of different analysts appeals to different realms of the patient's psyche. Nor can I imagine that this sort of "helpfulness" of the unconscious of the two parties, analyst and analysand, could be maintained throughout an entire analysis. The examination of transference and countertransference undertaken in Berlin, and especially the works of Blomeyer (1971) and myself (1971c) which describe how strongly the analyst's unconscious affects the process in the patient's psyche, speak decidedly against the hypothesis of obliging dreams.

Now I would like to clarify and discuss these theoretical hypotheses about symbols by examining a case example, that of a thirty-five-year-old female patient who started analytic therapy because of disorders in forming attachment to others, depressive moods, and symptoms of depersonalization. Not until the one hundredth hour did she write me a long letter confessing that she also suffered from a major, sensitive delusion of reference, and I had become a part of it. However, she had never decompensated to the point that she had to be admitted to a mental hospital or that she could no longer do her job as a secretary in an office.

As can be seen from his work on dementia praecox, Jung (1907/60) would have classified her suffering as a functional psychosis, especially as there was clearly a trigger situation to which I will refer later. In his last work on schizophrenia, Jung (1958/60) reported that when he moved from clinic to private practice he was astonished to find such compensated or latent psychoses much more often than he had expected, in a ratio of about one to ten, in fact. Today, we call such symptoms "borderline," but it is worth asking whether or not the old psychiatric diagnoses, such as "functional psychosis" (a term that Jung suggested) or the various severe neuroses rooted in developmentally early disturbances which are all included in the cumbersome group of borderline cases, would not be better described with the old terminology. A careful examination of Jung's works on schizophrenia reveals that he always treated such cases, some of them quite successfully. But only since the Freudians risked full-scale treatment of these disorders as well as the classical neuroses have the terminology and the problems called borderline become so popular. It has certainly been a serious failing on the part of Jungian analysts not to have taken up and developed Jung's clinical works in this area.

But let us return to the patient, Karin. During the whole first period of her therapy, a serious negative father complex occupied the foreground. Her father was a bricklayer and a heavy drinker who came from a family of drinkers (her grandfather and great grandfather were also alcoholics). She was the second child, born after a brother who was three years older than she, and unwanted because her mother had intended to leave her father before she had become pregnant again. From early on, her mother had reminded the patient of this rather brutally and treated her coldly and rejectingly. Therefore, Karin had had a closer relationship with her father, having had to fetch him home from the bar every Friday or at least go there in order to take the household money from him.

When he was completely drunk, the father had eruptions of aggressiveness at home and hit the mother and the brother. Little Karin was the only one who could calm him down a little by making him fried potatoes and putting him to bed. During puberty, he made sexual allusions to her, which made him more and more threatening and disgusting for Karin. Like most alcoholics, when he was sober he of course exhibited a soft, emotional, caring side. But this became evident only in the further course of the analysis, when she had come to a certain reconciliation with him. At first, he was only horrible, disgusting, and very frightening.

Immediately after the first interview, she brought the following initial dream to analysis:

> *A tiger has escaped from his cage through an open door. Detlef, my son, and I are fleeing from him. Suddenly we are standing in front of the empty cage, a long room. There is a door in the bars. It is open and we go through it. Driven by the terrible fear that the tiger could return, we run through the long cage to the other end, where we leave it through another little door. We lock the door of the cage with a key that we keep in our hands. Now we go to a little anteroom and look through the window. We are still terribly afraid. Suddenly the tiger is there. He is very big, terrible and fascinating. He does not take the same way as we did, but directly approaches our door. He wants to go into his cage, but we have locked the back door and hold the key in our hands. Now what? Suddenly the keeper comes and shouts, "Who's got the key?" I throw the key to him. Now the tiger goes past us and disappears behind the door. The keeper talks to him in a reassuring manner, and we hear him lock the cage door.*

In her monograph, "The Borderline Syndrome" (1972), Christa Rhode-Dachser pointed out that the initial dreams of these patients often contain motifs and symbols which are severely self- and world-destructive, an observation applicable to Karin, since the tiger threatened not only her with complete destruction but also her only child. These initial dream motifs are, of course, connected with the enormous aggressive destructiveness which lies in the psyches of these patients and which they cannot control. In most cases—as it was with my patient, too—it is not even directly repressed or completely unconscious but is coped with by the more archaic defense mechanism of active splitting.

So too, in the first period of the analysis, could I change from one moment to the next, from a good, protecting, and helping guardian into an evil tiger threatening to tear her apart. I do not want to go into these problems in detail here, but turn instead to the symbol of the tiger which, according to Karin's description, had distinctly mythological traits. I would like to deal with this symbol in regard to its status in the current situation as well as to its genesis, its further development during the treatment, and its relation to countertransference.

Her associations regarding the tiger came only with great hesitation, but all related to her father's alcoholism, about which she spoke most of the time during the early sessions. That the tiger referred to her father was also shown by a later dream in the first period of treatment in which she was in her parents' house together with her child and her mother, and the three of them waited anxiously for the tiger to come back while trying to protect themselves from him.

The great energy that lies in this powerful archaic animal—it spontaneously reminded me of the sabre-toothed tiger of the Paleozoic era—certainly has other components. In the dream, he is locked up in the cage after a short escape to freedom; this points to the systematized delusion Karin had withheld until the one hundredth hour and which contained such strong destructive energies. The systematized delusion referred to another field: to her own sexuality. Here again, there is a certain relation to the father since the daughter's first erotization in puberty, as we have already noted, came from him.

The systematized delusion had the following releasing stimulus: Karin's husband was a Dutchman who had volunteered to work in the former German Reich during the war and had stayed on afterward. In the first years following the war, he had worked as a tennis instructor, but after he married, he completely stopped working because of a minor case of tuberculosis. My very efficient patient provided for the family, and in addition they got some welfare money. After a short time, the husband became impotent, and Karin relieved her urgent sexual impulses by masturbating on the toilet. One day, while masturbating, she was surprised by her husband, who became morally very indignant with her. From that time on, he continually kept watch on her, even drilling a hole in the bathroom wall in order to observe her. (These events were real and not delusional. Since her husband had applied for analysis through public assistance, documents of his anamnesis existed which indicated that he had himself reported these events.)

Shortly afterward, Karin's sensitive delusion of reference broke out at her place of work. As she no longer dared to masturbate at home, she began masturbating in the washroom of her company when the urge became too strong. When she left the toilet, she met a worker who smiled cordially at her. She experienced this as a malicious grin: "He knew that I had masturbated and was making fun of me." Gradually she developed a paranoid system in which all her colleagues and her boss knew about her practice and continually hinted at it. It became so extreme that she interpreted certain traces in the dust in the stairwell as hints that revealed her misdemeanors. By the time she told me about her systematized delusion, I was already a part of it. She believed I had spoken to her boss, asked him to understand her, and promised improvement. Since then, the atmosphere in the company had improved a bit, and she was no longer exposed to so many torments. But, of course, this improvement did not last. The good father changed again into the evil one, and she reproached me for having told her dreams—especially the sexual ones—to all her co-workers in the company.

Thus in the symbol of the tiger two great fields are drawn together: the potential for strong aggression inherent in the alcoholism of her father and her sexuality. In his *Symbols of Transformation* (1912/56), Jung pointed out that women's images of wild animals, such as lions and tigers, often point toward the dynamics of sexual drives that cannot be controlled and are beyond the control of the ego. In this connection, a historical amplification is appropriate. At the time of Emperor Augustus, tigers became known and were transported to Europe for the first time. They were used for gladiatorial fights in the ancient Roman arena and later incorporated into artistic representations, especially on vases, where they were harnessed to the chariot of Amor or Dionysus. Thus they were regarded as the companion animals of the two gods who symbolize precisely those fields that created the greatest difficulties for my patient.

Now a question arises: What role did the transference situation at the beginning of analysis play in constellating this symbol? Every analysis is directed toward the unconscious and seeks to mobilize it. Because this is the unknown part of the personality and because the patient feels exposed to a mysterious medical procedure which is to a large extent unfamiliar, it is not surprising that dreams tinged with fears and anxieties appear. Moreover, Karin was confronted with a male analyst in this situation. With her severely negative father complex and very negative experiences, particularly with her father and her husband, it is no wonder that, in spite of the consciously friendly atmosphere, she experienced the analyst as split into a threatening tiger and a helping keeper.

But why an animal? At that time, I was not much older than Karin, and to her unconscious I must therefore have appeared as a potential sexual partner. The instinctual drive part of her sexuality was especially strongly repressed and very much under a moral taboo thanks to her decidedly prudish upbringing, which found blatant expression in her delusional symptom. But she also must have felt from the countertransference a much more permissive attitude and atmosphere regarding these areas than that to which she had been accustomed. Moreover, in our home we had a cat that related well to the whole family, moved freely about our apartment, and did not particularly respect my consultation room. The patient herself had never had any animals, and her attitude toward them tended to be fearful and negative. These facts may have played a role in her unconscious having chosen a dangerous big cat with which to make a first appearance.

In her examination of the conscious formation of symbols, Kreitler proves that they are formed in a gradual process with the help of other elements. She distinguishes ten elements, which we need not examine here, but in decreasing order of occurrence (with the first and second nearly equal), the most frequent sequences are:

1. scene, metaphor, symbol
2. metaphor, symbol
3. interpretation, metaphor, symbol
4. scene, symbol

In this connection it is interesting to note that there was an experience in Karin's childhood history that was obviously connected with the formation of the symbol. It was, of course, brought up later in the analysis; although not directly repressed, it had more or less fallen into oblivion. When she was between five and seven years old, she had performed a dance at a garden festival together with other children. She had the leading part and danced the part of a sunflower, dressed as a sunflower and holding a big sunflower in her hand. With this dance she was very successful with all the adults and children, and for a long time afterward people commented to her about it. It was a proud and special experience in her childhood. The sunflower has exactly the same colors as the tiger, and in the happy dance of the party there is the Dionysian element also found in the Roman use of the tiger to pull Dionysus's chariot. Here we have a positive side of the energy symbolized by the tiger: expansiveness, movement, creative play, and a happily successful representation in dance. What a pity, one might say, that Karin could not develop these possibilities, that they were suppressed and had wasted away and become rigid. It was only in analysis that she regained a small part of them.

Taking Kreitler's studies into consideration, the scene from childhood was the forerunner from which the symbol of the initial dream arose. It is, of course, only a hypothesis that the unconscious proceeds just like the conscious mind when forming a symbol, but I think it is probable. In Karin's case, the series of elements would be:

1. scene: the sunflower dance from childhood;
2. metaphor: father experienced as a tiger;
3. symbol: beyond its interpretation as father, the tiger takes on the much deeper meaning of an animalistic, elementary power that unites positive and negative aspects.

This was shown even more clearly in the further course of the analysis. As previously described, a sufficient holding (Winnicott 1958) was established around the one hundredth session following a positive transference dream in which she was cordially received as a guest in our home. She then found enough confidence in me to tell me in a long letter about her delusional system. A short time after this confession, she spontaneously began to express her inner world through a series of pictures whose production covered a period of two years.

The first picture of this series was closely connected to the central symbol of the initial dream. It showed Karin herself in the foreground as a dancer turned worshipfully toward a yellow sun, surrounded by billowing mists. In the background on the same stage was a man dressed as a magician who opened a curtain. Behind the curtain, a world could be seen, to which the magician was pointing. In the sky were the moon and stars, shining down upon the landscape.

The sunflower dance of her childhood was clearly recognizable in this picture, with a real sun in the sky this time. The paternal male figure was no longer a keeper who had to lock up something threatening, but rather a magician whom she associated with the analyst pointing to another world. The symbols of moon, stars, and landscape lent this world the distinct traits of a positive Great Mother. At that point, two things had obviously happened: the symbols of the father archetype had constellated positively and there appeared the sun as the ancient, positive, and life-giving symbol of divinity which she worshiped in a ritual dance. The senex was present in the figure of the wise magician who pointed to a world and a possibility of experience which had been, until then, denied to Karin because of the psychic "non-existence" of her personal mother. The symbol of the tiger was gone but, as we will see, it would reappear.

A short time before this, she had had another tiger dream in which the tiger moved about freely in the living room of her parents' house. Karin, her mother, and her son desperately tried to find shelter from him in another room. The tiger seemed still to have characteristics of the father, but it no longer appeared in an anonymous place; it had broken into her personal sphere. Since this dream occurred a short time before her confession, it may be assumed that the symbol had lost something of its threatening character. In the dream, at least, she could admit it into the same space with her, and at that point there might already have formed a vague suspicion that this symbol and the vital energies in it had other sides than those of the dismembering and dismembered Dionysus Zagreus.

About one year later, she had a dream which was decisive in the further development of this symbol in the analysis. In this dream, the patient danced through a whole series of cages of wild animals under the supervision and protection of an older man who only looked on. All these animals were big cats and the majority of them were tigers. Each time she danced into a cage, she was painfully pounced on by the animal in it, and each time she had an orgasm. Finally, after leaving the last cage, she sank to the ground, completely exhausted but also happy. There was still a little fear in the dream but much less than in earlier ones, and the pleasurable aspect of the experience clearly predominated.

Here we can clearly see how the dream ego can accept the positive, Dionysian side of the erotic sexual experience. It is also important that here again there were cages, that is, enclosed and protected places for orgiastic experience. The figure of the senex belongs in this context, as he obviously supervised the whole event and seemed able to intervene at any time in a helpful manner if things had gotten out of hand. With borderline cases and psychoses—of which I will speak later—the symbols of the complex core have a very high energy charge, and they always threaten to inflate the often unstable conscious ego. I believe that this danger was avoided because of the protected place in which the instinctual action took place. In *Psychology and Alchemy* (1952), Jung described a dream in which a reptile touched the dreamer in the course of his attempt "to become." Jung associated this animal life form with the totality of the innate unconscious, which is to be united with consciousness. In order to carry out this transformation, one has to let oneself be bitten by wild animals without running away from them. This means being able to expose oneself to the instinctual impulses of the unconscious without identifying with them or having them flee back into the unconscious.

It is important and interesting that the delusions in Karin's consciousness changed in a manner precisely parallel with the development of the symbols. After her confession, and after having painted the first picture with the sun and moon symbols, the patient provoked an argument with her boss at the company, whereupon she was dismissed. Since she was an efficient and diligent worker, she had no difficulty finding a new job immediately where she was even better paid. In this way, she broke out of the delusional masturbatory atmosphere and left behind the delusion that all around her could tell by looking at her that she had masturbated and persecute her because of it. In its place, she developed a systematized delusion that she had become homosexual. She reproached the analyst for having turned her into a homosexual. She did have some dreams of a homosexual character, and since dream and reality were not sufficiently separated from each other in her experience, for her this meant that she really was a manifest homosexual, for which she utterly despised herself. (I should emphasize that this took place at a time when male homosexuality was still punishable by law in West Germany and lesbianism was much more taboo than it is today.)

Then, for the first time in the analysis, Karin manifested aggressions against her mother and experienced deep feelings of envy toward her brother, whom her mother had always preferred. She found expression for her deep indignation as well at the fact that her mother had told her with such cruelty that she had been a completely unwanted child. Concurrently, her father took on more positive traits. She recalled times when she had gotten along well with him.

The next phase began after her dream of the cages. She had come to accept her sexuality then, and the passive delusions that referred to it disappeared almost completely. But now she discovered that everyone she looked at—on the street, in the subway, in her workplace, or in a shop—blushed. When I asked her why that happened, she said, "They think I'm a woman who throws herself at them." Simultaneously, she began for the first time to doubt the reality of her delusion. She heard an inner voice saying to her, "It can't be like that. Either everybody else is crazy, or I'm crazy. Since everybody else can't be crazy, probably I'm crazy." This last symptom is erythrophobia, projected onto other persons. Behind these symptoms are predominantly latent aggressive and self-abandonment tendencies. It seemed to me that a new relation to the people around her opened up and now included men. The further course of therapy confirmed this.

Looking at Karin's various systematized delusions from the perspective of her ability to make contact with and relate to other people, one could outline the sequence in which the various delusions followed each other:

1. Masturbation: I relate only to myself; I am totally alone and do not want any contact except with myself.
2. Homosexuality: I try to establish a relationship with another woman.
3. Erythrophobia: I also include men in the circle of persons to whom I want to relate.

This sketch is not intended to be an explanatory formula for these three terms, which are, of course, much more inclusive in their contents. It is only an attempt to view the sequence of symbols in this patient from a particular point of view.

The symbol of the tiger reappeared in a very changed form only after several years and at the end of her therapy. In contrast to her earlier withdrawal into defiant silence, Karin had argued with me aggressively. The strong aggression reminded me again of the dismembering tiger, and her aggression often was hard to bear in the countertransference. She painted—or, better, let come into being on paper—a lotus blossom surrounded by yellow beams of light. In its center were the moon and stars surrounded by a red circle. In her words, the yellow beams represented the setting sun. The systematized delusion had disappeared in the meantime. With the symbol of the lotus blossom, the self had also constellated as a symbol of wholeness, a psychic wholeness in which the wild animal was obviously included.

In contrast to Kernberg (1975), I have never been able to decide, when working with borderline patients or patients with psychoses, whether it is necessary to introduce an analytic rule forbidding strongly aggressive verbal attacks on the person of the analyst. Kernberg is certainly right in stating that in such cases the likelihood of countertransference aggression increases, especially since these patients usually command very good intuition which enables them to grasp and exploit vulnerabilities in the analyst. In my experience, I believe it better to endure this aggression and then to utilize the countertransference aggression at an appropriate moment to show my annoyance or hurt, but at the same time to convey to the patient that he cannot completely destroy our relationship with his uncontrolled aggressiveness. I think the borderline patient needs to encounter at least one person who can not only understand him, but also accept his tiger.

Before returning to the problem of the complex core and its symbols, I would like to say a few final words about Karin's therapy. More or less by chance, I saw her again after twenty years when she needed a short consultation because her son was in the phase of separation from her. In all these years, she had not developed any systematized delusions and had made it without any further therapy, something which, in my experience, occurs only rarely. But it would be presumptuous to say that she had been cured. She remained a quite paranoid personality. After the separation from her husband, from who she never succeeded in breaking off all contact, she did not establish any other stable partner relationship. Nevertheless, I think that the therapy gave her a lot and that without treatment she probably would have ended up in a mental hospital or would have completely isolated herself from the world. She also would not have been able successfully to raise her son without having him fall victim to a serious neurosis.

I would like to deal now with a question that concerns the libidinization of the central symbols of a complex core. Of course, I am using *libido* in the sense analytical psychology makes of the term, as an unspecified energy. Most of the analysts of the Freudian school start from the idea—influenced by newer findings on ego psychology—that the borderline syndrome can be etiologically attributed to a specific disorder of the ego which has affected the whole system of the psychic "apparatus." Together with others, such authors as Kernberg (1975), Green (1975), Jacobson (1964), and Modell (1963) are preeminent. Others, such as Wollberg (1968), for example, oppose this conception of ego deficiency since it discriminates against the borderline just as it does against the organic psychotic and could support a therapeutic nihilism. In contrast to this view, one can assume the presence of a relatively stable ego that is disturbed by a highly differentiated pattern of defense reactions, with the cognitive functions and perception especially affected. But Wollberg's conception, too, focuses primarily on disorders of the ego structure acquired in early childhood and makes only passing reference to the possibility that certain constitutional weaknesses of the ego structure could also play a part.

Following Jung's lead, I come back to a concept which I mentioned initially. I think that the energetic power of the complex that appears in the symbol dominates "a more or less unstable ego." In all his work in this field, Jung dealt with a problem to which the Freudians paid practically no attention. Time and again he raised the question: "Is there a toxin unknown to us in the genetic coding that provokes an intensified activity of the unconscious?" (In the beginning, Jung presumed that there was a chemical or hormonal influence.) In such a situation, an ego that actually is "normal" and sufficiently developed would be overwhelmed and inflated by the powerful energy of an unconscious complex. I think it is essential that we analytical psychologists again take up and pursue this idea. As any experienced analyst knows, this question is all the more important considering we meet a lot of patients who do not react to serious or very severe early disorders with borderline symptoms or a psychosis at all. There are many cases of simple neuroses where a long and differentiated analysis reveals early disorders which equal or exceed those of borderline patients in their quality and quantity. I would even presume that there are a great number of so-called "sane" people in our society who suffer exactly the same early disorders but have never fallen clinically ill or shown any conspicuous symptoms or needed therapy.

As early as 1907, in his work on dementia praecox, Jung (1907/60) emphasized that these emotional complexes have enormous power. He pointed out that such complexes have the same constellating effect on the remaining psychic activities as acute affect. Everything that suits the complex is accepted and all the rest is excluded, or at least inhibited. As a demonstration of this mechanism, he cites the familiar example of religious ideas. Today we recognize that this mechanism can be found not only in religion but in politics, science, technology, and economics as well. Are we perhaps all borderlines, or do we all have a borderline person in us who appears time and again in our consciousness with complex-obsessed ideas? (I have dealt in detail with this highly offensive idea elsewhere (Dieckmann 1987b).)

In the same essay of 1907, Jung discusses the possibility that the correcting voices which can be found in some of these patients might represent the "repressed normal remnants of the ego complex" breaking through into consciousness. Similarly, there is clinical evidence that prematurely demented people can function again with sufficient normality when they have a serious physical illness. In all these cases, there must have already existed a sufficiently well-structured ego-complex. Today, of course, we know from psychosomatics that these serious physical illnesses represent repressions into the somatic. At this point, the theory would be contradicted: if the borderline patient is able to repress so strongly that he can work with a more mature defense mechanism than he ought to have developed, there must be something wrong with the whole theory.

In this connection, the voice Karin heard telling her that the others could not all be crazy and that there must be something wrong with her own perceptions seems to support the argument that more mature parts of the ego-complex can arise in certain situations. One could, of course, raise the objection that the voice she heard was a result of the success of the therapy in facilitating a bit of ego formation or maturation. But one can just as easily argue the opposite and advance the hypothesis that the success of the therapy lay in the fact that the patient had been enabled to follow this voice and that the energy of the pathogenic complex had diminished. I will return to this later, since the energy invested in the complexes and their symbols is an important part of my thoughts.

In the preface to the second edition of "Contents of the Psychoses" (1914/60), Jung again wrote of a hereditary disposition or a toxin of unknown nature that could bring into being a nonadjusted psychological function which could develop into illness with the corresponding releasing stimulus. But as early as 1911, in his essay, "A Criticism of Bleuler's Theory of Schizophrenic Negativism" (1911/60, p. 245), Jung explained in great detail why this problem should not be dealt with as though it stems from a single source—either psychic or organic—but rather by reference to a multifactorial "conditionalism." In his view, most people who suffer from dementia praecox had an innate tendency toward psychic conflicts. They have an abnormal irritability (today, we would say an extreme sensibility), and their conflicts therefore differ from normal tensions in their emotional intensity. Their conflicts bring them into a state of panic, a chaos of emotions and strange thoughts. At this point, we have to be aware of the fact that many of the cases which Jung described with the term *dementia praecox* would today be classified as borderline.

In his last work on schizophrenia, Jung described this dilemma, as he called it, in a more modern form:

> [A]re we to assume, as a causal factor, a weakness of the ego-personality, or a particularly strong affect? I regard the latter hypothesis as the more promising, and for the following reason. The notorious weakness of ego-consciousness in the sleeping state means next to nothing so far as a psychological understanding of the dream-contents is concerned. It is the feeling-toned complex that determines the meaning of the dream, both dynamically and also as regards its content. We must undoubtedly apply this criterion to schizophrenia, for, so far as we can see at present, the whole phenomenology of this disease turns on the pathogenic complex. In our attempts at explanation we shall probably do best if we start from this point and regard the weakening of the ego-personality as secondary, as one of the destructive concomitants of a feeling-toned complex which arose under normal conditions but afterwards shattered the unity of the personality by its intensity. (Jung 1958/60, p. 269)

Here Jung clearly takes the view that there is an excessive strength of affect and not an excessive weakness of the ego. I took the same view in the beginning of this essay, especially in my fourth thesis concerning the level of energy of archetypal symbols. When we consider Karin's case, I believe one can speak neither of an excessive weakness of the ego nor of a dominance of the archaic defense formations such as active splitting (Kernberg 1975) and projective identification (Klein 1946). Both of these defense mechanisms could certainly be found in this patient, too, but they were not stronger than in cases of neurosis. I would even say that splitting as well as projective identification continue to exist as archaic forms of defense even in healthy persons and that they become visible in situations especially colored by affect. In an essay on enemy images (Dieckmann 1984), I showed that it is quite common to use these defenses on a collective level as an almost malicious sort of party game.

Apart from these archaic defenses, my patient had much more mature defense formations at her disposal, and the extent of her repression was certainly larger and more extensive. Furthermore, I would not say that she had a very unstable ego-complex. It is really quite an accomplishment to withhold a systematized delusion for one hundred sessions of analysis. Furthermore, she was able to react discreetly to the people about her, and in spite of her paranoid fears she never completely destroyed her relationships with her colleagues. Of course, she warded off a lot by means of avoidance but this, too, is seen as a mature rather than as an archaic defense mechanism. I would not attribute to the patient a mature and adequately functioning ego, but rather question the theory of an ego weakness acquired in early childhood in favor of an especially intense strength of complex in borderline patients.

The libidinal intensity of Karin's symbols was especially impressive, but also hard to describe. There was such energy coming from them that I felt as though the tiger was actually in the room. We also sometimes find such an intensity when dealing with archetypal dreams or active imagination in the therapy of a neurosis. But this is an exception, and the powerful energetic tensions that come from the unconscious and the characteristically long periods of therapy in borderline cases differ considerably from therapy with an average neurosis.

In 1965, Rosemary Gordon dealt with the idea that projective identification has by no means only negative effects but is capable of breaking down limits within the person concerned as well as in the object world, which can be essential for qualitative changes in the structure of the personality (Gordon 1965, p. 145). In the same essay, she stated that what Jung understood as *participation mystique* ("unconscious identity, psychic infection and inductions") were synonymous with projective identification (ibid., p. 128). I have to confess that I have a certain dislike for the term *projective identification* and prefer the term *participation mystique*. It seems to me that the former is too strongly connected to the patriarchal heroic ego of Occidental culture and emphasizes too heavily the distinction (which is also an active split) between the healthy analyst and the deplorably ill neurotic. Almost all Freudian authors describe it as a one-sided transaction wherein the patient invests in the analyst. When a countertransference projective identification occurs from analyst to patient, it is almost always viewed as a pathologically disturbing process. I prefer the cross-cousin marriage model of transference that Jung developed in "The Psychology of the Transference" (1946/54b). According to this model, such processes on the lower level of the unconscious transference between the anima of the (male) analyst and the animus of the (female) patient are considered normal and important for therapy. (In my book *Methods in Analytical Psychology* (1991), I too emphasized the therapeutic importance of this axis.)

I would like to give a clear example from the therapy of a thirty-two-year-old borderline patient. He was an eternal student who had studied mathematics for twenty-four semesters without taking any qualifying examinations. He had been in mental hospitals several times and had been treated there with shock therapy, even though his diagnosis was serious compulsion neurosis with moderate paranoid ideation. He lived almost completely in a dimension between outer reality and fantasy strongly mystical in its orientation. I would call it a deformed *mundus imaginalis* as described by Corbin (1979). In many archetypal dreams, highly charged with emotion, this *mundus imaginalis* also had the character of an absolute psychic reality, with the corresponding projective identifications into the world about him.

To one of his sessions, the patient brought the following dream:

> *It turns out that Hitler is not dead and takes power in Germany again. As I have dark hair and a hooked nose, the SS regards me as a Jew, and they throw me in prison. I am completely in despair and try to affirm my innocence. I do not succeed. Some days later, an SS officer comes to my dungeon and tells me that he is now going to kill me with a shot in the neck. He pulls out his pistol, and I wake up trembling all over.*

The patient was twenty minutes late, and when he greeted me, his hands were wet with sweat. Trembling, he dropped onto the couch and told me that I was the SS officer in disguise and that he really expected me to pull out a pistol and shoot him. To me, it was a miracle that he had mustered the courage to come at all. He had obviously projected his own aggressive maleness onto me and now expected that I would act accordingly and free him from his severe guilt feelings caused by his excessive narcissistic contempt for others.

At first, I was amazed and at a loss for what to do, all the more so as I knew that the patient did not respond at all to reality control. But then something remarkable happened in me. I had the strong feeling that I was a mother holding my own little baby in my arms—myself, not the patient—who was terrified through and through. I started to make swaying motions with the upper part of my body and to utter nonverbal, calming sounds. By projective counteridentification, I had displaced my own baby onto the patient. And it was exactly this process that calmed the patient down little by little so that by the end of the hour he could say with a sigh of relief, "It must have been a dream."

In such situations, I ask myself if we really have to adopt all our clinical terms from the Freudians. Would it not be much more appropriate to use the term *participation mystique*, which is much more in accord with our theory of complex constellations in which both the analyst and the patient take part? On the basis of my experience, I simply do not believe that there can be a one-sided projective identification except with very schizoid analysts, although the analyst's contribution can differ greatly from one analyst to another. The hook on which a projection hangs might be large or small, but there is always a hook.[2]

---

[2]Here I would like to mention the brilliant work of Nathan Schwartz-Salant, "Archetypal Foundations of Projective Identification" (1986), which has given me many valuable insights.

Before dealing again with symbols, I must make a few additional remarks concerning my basic concept. In my opinion, the clinical theory of complexes has not been further developed since Jung's time, at least not in an integrated form and not with regard to the various clinical syndromes. Complexes are, of course, often mentioned by Jungians, and new complexes are quite often found and described, but not usually in their clinical interconnections. In most cases, they are amplified and examined with regard to the variety of their symbols. These studies certainly are valuable, and I have no intention of downplaying them. But I think there is a lacuna in analytical psychology in regard to a more modern theory of complexes that can be used in clinical diagnostics as well as in therapy by individual analysts. We all need a basic instrument that enables us to understand the essential outlines of the formations and intricate, highly variable patterns of experience in the psyche of our patients. Time and again, we see that in both general and specific theories of neuroses, Jungians have to fall back on the positions of Freudian psychoanalysis, especially when we are dealing with the therapy of the personal unconscious. I find this both regrettable and unnecessary, since complex theory puts at our disposal something more modern than the concept of the "psychic apparatus" with its dominance of today's ego-psychology where the unconscious gets short-changed. I appreciate the Freudian positions and their further development and do not want to attack them, and I have not the least objection to including and utilizing them. I think only that we should make more use of our own possibilities in this area.

Within the scope of a seminar held for many years at the C. G. Jung Institute of Berlin, where we have been dealing intensively with urgent ecological problems that today threaten the survival of humankind as a whole, I have noticed certain parallels between the microcosm and the macrocosm. In my view, the complex structure of the human psyche resembles the ecological self-regulation in nature surrounding us. Therefore, it should be possible to develop a systems theory of psychic complexes. Based on the case I have been discussing, I will attempt to comment on the interconnections among the complexes. The two great parental complexes as well as their core elements—for example, the senex, the hero, the old wise woman, the witch, and so on—are regulatory centers in relationship with one another and experience a free interchange of libido in a sufficiently functional psyche.[3]

It might seem a bit confusing that I speak of one great complex on the one hand and of several complex cores on the other. But empirical clinical expe-

---

[3]I will illustrate this utilizing two diagrams of Karin's complexes that were mobilized at the beginning and at the end of therapy (see figs. 8.1 and 8.2 at the end of the chapter).

rience with such a scheme of pyramids shows that, in the case of a psychic disturbance, for example, of the father complex, only a very few of the archetypal points are mobilized or energized. In Karin's case, there were only the predatory mythological father at the animal level and the violent senex at the human level. Furthermore, they are partly or completely dissociated from the ego-complex and thus form complex cores of their own which are, so to speak, split off from the larger context of the father complex.

These two great basic complexes must be juxtaposed by the third element, the ego-complex with all its functions as well as its conscious and unconscious components. It is, of course, connected to the shells as well as to the cores of the complexes. This results in a triangulation which might form a bridge between schools, since nowadays the Freudians are known to deal more fequently with the preoedipal processes that Jung pointed out early on.

This is a brief and very incomplete sketch of what I have in mind. Within our ecology work group, we have been dealing especially with the nature of collective confrontation in terms of mythology, history, and contemporary events. In a certain sense, this work has formed the basis for a systems theory of the complexes.

First, however, I would like to give a further example of symbol formation, also from a borderline patient whose case I have presented elsewhere (Dieckmann 1971b). The patient is a forty-five-year-old woman with periods of severe depression, states of mental confusion, and a series of suicide attempts. During the first period of analysis, she was dominated by a pronounced negative mother complex. Her strong feelings of hate for her mother were accompanied by equally violent feelings of guilt. She had grown up abroad where both parents did missionary work for a severe and restrictive sect. The mother was the second wife of her father, who already had two daughters from his first marriage, but after the death of his first wife, he had entrusted the girls to foster parents. In this second marriage, my patient Ruth was the second of five children. As both parents were always traveling because of their missionary work, she and a sister two years older were left almost entirely with native servants. When Ruth was six years old, the family went to Europe on a holiday, during which the mother did not stay with the children, but traveled in various countries giving lectures on her missionary work. "Service to God," they told their two daughters, "is more important than taking care of one's own children."

When they went abroad again, the two daughters were deemed a burden and given without further ado to a member of their sect with whom they were to stay for the next eight years. To make matters worse, this man was a chance acquaintance. Ruth's older sister did not survive this treatment. Shortly before the parents' departure, she developed a serious case of pneumonia and died. Ruth's remaining childhood and adolescence were nothing but suffering. Her foster mother was no better than her own and must have had severely sadistic traits. She was finally able to escape from this situation only by marrying very early against her mother's wishes. But in the meantime, she had introjected the negative mother imago and was partly identified with it, bearing five children as her own mother had. In part, she developed a counterposition by leading a veritable Cinderella existence within her marriage.

When I met her, she looked like a gray, evangelical church mouse and a living symbol of the abandoned and ignored child. But she had—and this surely had saved her life—a great vitality. In addition, she was endowed with a distinctly above average intelligence and a capacity for creativity, which had been latent to a large extent. From the beginning of the analysis, she tried to express herself and her problems in a creative manner. At first, she did it in the form of long written compositions and poems, then in drawings and paintings as well as sculpted works in clay. The latter led to the first decisive symbol formations in the analysis.

In one of her initial dreams, she went through a dirty kitchen to a room in a deserted house where many abandoned, ill, and half-starved children were lying about. As I have already noted in reference to such patients, she did not experience this dream as an event in the *mundus imaginalis* but rather as an external reality which demanded her immediate help. Consequently she decided to adopt a black child even though three of her five children were still little and she had to care for them. Of course, the family did not have much money. It was very difficult for me to dissuade her from acting on her plan, and I was finally able to do so only by referring to the analytic ground rule that projects decisive for a patient's life can be undertaken only when both sides accept them and when they are appropriately worked through analytically.

Barely half a year after beginning analysis, the following fantasy developed and returned time and again:

> I feel myself being carried in the arms of a big, strong, primitive man. Sometimes, he is black! He doesn't pay any attention to me personally, but only wants me as a woman. After a long battle, he overcomes me because actually I want him to overcome me, too. At this moment my whole femininity suddenly awakes. I need this male strength and I need to be overcome by the masculine to be able to have an orgasm at all. If this doesn't happen, I quite literally remain dry.

I was rather astonished by this graphic report from a patient who, up to that moment, had been quite prudish and had not spoken at all about sexuality. In spite of the libidinal charge, she experienced this fantasy for the first time in the space of her own inner, creative process, and shortly afterward she started to model in clay. Of course, she wanted to make the black man, but something else happened. She told me about it in the following session in these words:

> My depression of the last few days is not yet entirely gone. But it has gotten better. I feel like I am caught in a spider web. I had the need to shape something in clay. I had to overcome a strong resistance to do what I wanted to and what would help me. I didn't have any idea how to start. Of course, I thought the whole time about my beautiful black man and how I could form him. But I was simply blocked. So I just kneaded the moist clay for about half an hour with my fingers and observed the shapes that appeared. I saw heads of animals, I felt the cool clay, and finally I stopped thinking entirely. Then I suddenly saw how the shape of a child arose as if out of the earth. This child had a toothache. It ran to its mother and buried its aching head between her breasts. This suffering child is still very much alive in me today.

She brought this figure with her to the session, and I must admit that I was astonished at the artistic form and the powerful expression it had. It was the first sculpted work she had ever made. In contrast to the dream—she said herself—this time she experienced the sick child as her own inner figure. The comforting mother who can take the sick and abandoned child within into her comforting arms and who no longer has "dry" breasts had developed in her own inner world and was now experienced consciously as an important symbol.

The process by which this symbol arose was by no means spontaneous. A half hour of intensive psychic work was needed to push aside the figure of the black man who was dominating her consciousness. Only then did the process gradually begin in which the symbol of the positive mother archetype with the child developed out of the material. Just as in Karin's case, for Ruth, the symbol took up an early childhood experience without which I cannot imagine it originating. The kind mother figure corresponds to an Asian wet nurse in whose care Ruth had spent her first six years of life. She became clearly recognizable in the figures Ruth formed later. To her astonishment, these figures had Asian traits, but I had to draw her attention to them. Only relatively late in the analysis did the figure of this wet nurse, which had been repressed, return to consciousness. Here we have a process of symbol formation similar, indeed almost identical, to the one observed in Karin's case.

There are countless definitions of the symbol in the literature. There are anthropological, theological, mythological, philosophical, as well as mystical, artistic, and psychological definitions. The psychological definitions in particular differ enormously and derive certain elements from all the other areas listed. But I would like to keep to C. G. Jung's definition, which I have altered a bit, but which raises a clinically important question: Does the symbol become a symbol only when it is acknowledged or experienced as such by consciousness? Is it really—as I described it in Karin's case—first scene, then metaphor? Does the tiger become a symbol only when he appears in the picture as sun and senex and when Karin goes through the cages? Rather, is it not that the tiger is already a symbol in the initial dream, just as the sunflower dance already was? Do not all these inner, imaginal experiences produce considerable effects on consciousness and the psyche such as can be caused only by a genuine symbol?

We can probably answer all these questions in the affirmative, and perhaps it is better not to speak of the origin or the creation of symbols but rather of the process by which a symbol becomes conscious or is consciously recognized. But this seems to me to be of decisive therapeutic importance, particularly with borderline or psychotic cases. Let us again look at what happened when both patients consciously understood the symbol as metaphor or almost as a sign. For Karin, the tiger was the potentially extremely aggressive, drunken father of whom she was enormously afraid. As a child she had to handle him and be his keeper. Now her dream ego is allowed to flee from him, and she withdraws into secrecy, fear, mistrust, and defiant silence. Although she certainly needed this period, I am reluctant to regard it as a positive regression. Rather, I have the feeling that the mobilization of the complex in the beginning phase strengthened her resistances. With Ruth, the situation was very similar. The metaphor of the sick child in the dream almost led to adopting a black child and hence to an intensification of her masochism that would have been irremediable. Her resistance found expression in her absolute wish to act out. She filled entire sessions trying to convince me.

But at the moment when each of them became aware of the realm of inner symbols and were able to understand the tiger and the child as such, their conditions changed. Karin's systematized delusion, rigid up until that time, began to break up, and Ruth was able to turn to her inner world and to some extent avoid acting out. On the basis of our analytic knowledge, we cannot simply say that symbols will exert their healing effect regardless whether or not one understands them. Such an attitude, which only sees the prospective sides of symbols that come from the unconscious, can be more dangerous than helpful to severely disturbed patients. Symbols have not only a healing character but can, when misunderstood, impede treatment or significantly worsen a condition. In fact, there is nothing that defenses and resistances cannot misuse for their purposes.

Symbols can become active within the transcendent function only when the defense systems are loosened up to the extent that they allow symbolic understanding and experience into consciousness. We might put it more cautiously and speak of the permission for other possibilities of experiencing and understanding than have corresponded heretofore to the complex-fixated schemas. This facilitates the increase in libido available to the ego-complex and to consciousness. But not all the libido bound up in a complex is transferred to consciousness by the analytic process—to the extent that it is successful—to be at the disposal of the ego-complex. If we take Karin's tiger seriously as a real inner tiger with all the strength and energy inherent in it, as Hillman (1979) does phenomenologically in his book on dreams, the result of our therapy would be a sort of superhuman whose consciousness would have a gigantic energy potential at its disposal. Borderline and psychotic patients in particular can teach us that there are enormous energies in the complexes. In successful analytic processes, something else happens in the unconscious that I would call a distribution of energy. As Verena Kast (1986) puts it, every symbol always retains a surplus of meaning.

One last dream that Karin had shortly before concluding her analysis may clarify this. At this time, after four years of therapy and more than five hundred hours of treatment, she felt relatively well, and by and large she was coping relatively well with her life on her own. In this dream, she was standing in a circus arena which had a fence around it as is usual when wild animals are being trained. Through a passageway three tigers entered this arena. She is afraid of them and shrinks back toward the exit. The tamer enters the arena through this exit and indicates that she should leave it while he holds the tigers back.

No major changes followed this dream, but it became more and more apparent that her analysis was moving toward the end. The symbol had by no means dissolved but rather was preserved just as it had appeared in the initial dream. Now, however, an experienced man in a protected space handled these animals and knew how to treat them. With the necessary respect and the appropriate distance in the dream and from the unconscious, she was now able to experience the positive and negative, destructive and creative elements of this mythological father animal. Although Karin did not understand this dream and neither could nor wanted to translate it, it meant a great deal to her, and she recalled it often during the remainder of her therapy. In the meantime, her consciousness had developed an understanding and respect for symbolic experience.

If we review these two case examples from the viewpoint of the development of the symbolism, it seems to me that something happens here that we could compare with the regeneration of an ecotype that has been overgrown and poisoned by one species. Both Karin and Ruth were initially dominated by a single complex. In Karin's case, it was the negative father complex, and in Ruth's case the negative mother complex. To a large extent, these two complexes determined all experiential and behavioral modes of the entire psyche, not only of the conscious ego-complex. A shift of energy, and therefore a mobilization of other complex cores, occurred in the course of therapy. If we review this again in Karin's case, we get the following picture.

At first, the unconscious mobilized a mythological father animal which also potentially contained positive elements of the father archetype but which could not yet be accepted by consciousness. Then, through the picture she painted, the white or positive magician enters the drama as an archetype and therewith the father god as the sun, the light-bringer, the Great Round. For his part, the white magician obviously points via his anima toward the earth archetype of the Great Mother and toward the feminine Great Round, the moon in the nocturnal starry sky. In the next step, which again is accompanied by a positive fatherly senex figure, a direct contact with the dismembering animal occurs. This leads to an acceptance of sexuality and of Dionysian experience as well as a gradual increase in personal memories of her father, among which there are many positive ones. The personal father is no longer only black but has become black and white. Finally, at the end, the figure of the animal tamer appears, who, in my view, should be classified with the archetype of culture hero, since he is able to tame the animal powers and to use them creatively.

I have followed this line for certain complex cores that belong to the father archetype and only hinted at the bridge to the mother archetype. Of course, the mother archetype in Karin's case was treated just as extensively, and using this bridge to other dreams and changes in the patient's experience, one could demonstrate how the various complex cores in the mother archetype were also filled out or better put, were included in this cycle. Although I have gone more into the formation of the symbol in Ruth's case, we can recognize the same process at work. Here the dominating, negative personal mother is supplemented symbolically by a positive, archetypal mother figure, a Demeter-Kore symbol, in which the mother and the daughter merge. The event that triggered the formation of this symbol was her search for her own femininity in transpersonal sexuality, with which the unconscious apparently did not want to have anything to do and rather sought out its own path. Only much later in Ruth's therapy, when she remembered her Asian wet nurse, did an upwelling of positive personal experiences with mothers occur. Her own mother remained negative throughout the entire therapy, although at the end Ruth no longer hated her but was able to understand her to a certain extent. I will not go into detail here, but in this therapy the various symbolizations or personifications of the archetypal cores of the mother and the father complexes were also filled out and libidinally mobilized. In this case, too, there occurred a division and distribution of energy to the various complexes with which the ego-complex was able to establish contact.

In his scheme of pyramids in *Aion*, Jung (1959) sketched a structure of the self archetype, finally bringing the four pyramids into a circle. This circle could be understood as the great circular system embracing the entire psyche. In my opinion, we could draw similar or equivalent pyramidal models for the cores of the father and the mother complexes. To the extent that it is not treasonous, one would have to include personal elements.[4]

I consider such pyramidal models as self-regulating systems, meaningful and useful to the extent that, applied to the father and the mother archetypes, they can give us a map showing what specific personifications of the complex core are energized and which components are excluded and not experienced in the first interview and at the beginning of therapy. Then, in the course of and at the end of treatment, these schemes can show what could be filled, enlivened, or revivified during therapy. A scheme for the case of Karin is shown in figures 8.1 and 8.2. In her case, at the beginning there existed only the negative father and man, that is, the lower point of transition between the first and the second pyramids. By way of the mythological father animal of the third pyramid (situated relatively deep in the unconscious) and a more negative senex of the second pyramid (the keeper), the father god (sun) and the positive senex (magician) were mobilized. Then the father's anima led to the activation of the mother archetype, and finally a positive hero figure appeared at the end. As far as I can observe in this case, no relation to the level of the fourth (elementary) pyramid was established. Perhaps this is why a rather strong paranoid element in Karin's personality did not disappear.

---

[4]I rest my view on Mary Williams's (1963) statement regarding the indivisibility of the personal and the collective unconscious. Elsewhere (Dieckmann 1986) I discuss in detail how useful it is to include in our theory certain personal elements from early childhood in the core element of the complex and not restrict them only to the shell of the complex.

FIGURE 8.1 *Example of the Father Archetype*
Karin at the start of therapy

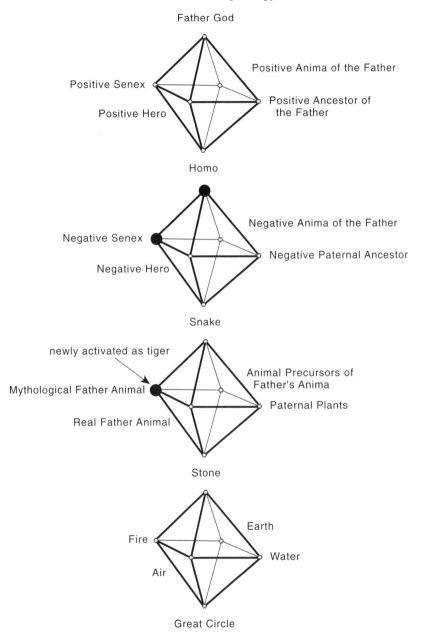

FIGURE 8.2 Structure of Archetypes
Karin at the end of therapy

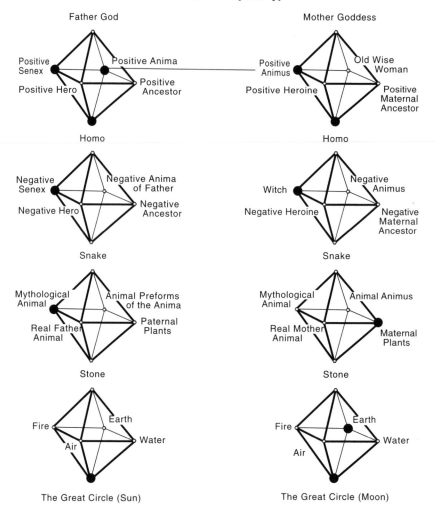

The Great Circle (Sun)   The Great Circle (Moon)

CHAPTER 9

The Oedipus Complex in Analytical Psychology

Surely no book about complexes can be written without discussing the world-famous Oedipus complex, which analytical psychology accepts and acknowledges, although not as the sole complex in the human psyche, the overcoming of which forms the basis for all healthy psychic functioning. In analytical psychology, the Oedipus complex is one among many, an important one, of course, and it has moreover an additional significance insofar as it draws in all of mythology as well as the origins of mythology rooted in the transition from matriarchy to patriarchy.

Thanks to Freud, probably no other Greek myth is as well known in our culture as Sophocles' version of the myth of Oedipus. One could say that the Oedipus of Sophocles has become a sort of complex core for Occidental civilization. Psychodynamically, we must infer that a complex that so rapidly pervades a given culture with such violent positive or negative affect has to be touching a central problem and hence an archetype constellated in the culture. At least in the threefold significance of patricide, mother-son incest, and the subsequent self-castration as punishment, Freud himself elevated the Oedipus complex to the level of significance for all human beings and made it the central complex in all human development. It is only against this last assertion that analytical psychology raises objections which crystallize around three points:

1) It is impermissible to accent the myth only in terms of the sexual-incestuous libido, since the story is primarily about a power complex which, in its oldest form, reaches back into the time of transition from the matriarchy to the patriarchy. In older myth, the figure of Oedipus belongs to the year kings whose ancestors were slain at the end of the year, and whose successors then married the high priestess of the mother goddess (Ranke-Graves 1960).

2) Even in our culture, the Oedipus complex is only one complex among many that can be constellated in the course of the psychic develop-

ment of the individual. Even early on, after he had intensively investigated the mythologies of various peoples, Jung (1912/56) recognized that the libido moved from the sexual to the nutritive functions as regression deepened, and that the language of simile and metaphor also underwent a transformation into the imagery of the alimentary functions such that the Jonah-and-the-whale complex took the place of the Oedipus complex. In this transformation, incest anxiety changed into fear of being eaten or devoured.

3) The Oedipus complex is not valid for all cultures, but rather specific to our culture. Stein (1974) has pointed out that there are many primal peoples who do not have an incest taboo vis à vis the parents but only in regard to siblings. We can no longer denigrate this as something primitive and preoedipal, as was done in the nineteenth and early twentieth centuries; rather, we know today, thanks to extensive ethnological studies, that the so-called "primitive" peoples were not at all primitive but had developed areas other than natural science and technology. In these areas, they were just as differentiated and, in part, superior to us, as Lévi-Strauss (1966) has shown.

I will attempt to elaborate these three points further. In order to emphasize that the Oedipus complex is not simply an incest trauma inspired by the sole wish to marry mother and kill father and to be castrated for this crime, let us first turn to the origin of the actual story. According to Willamowitz-Moellendorf (1919), the god Apollo revealed to Laius, the king of Thebes, that he would bear a son with his wife Iocasta, and this son would slay him. According to Ranke-Graves (1960), Laius queried the oracle at Delphi, which announced to him that the child Iocasta would bear him would be his murderer. Hearing this, he rejected Iocasta without giving her any reason for his decision. This angered her so much that she got him drunk and as soon as night fell lured him into her arms. When a son was born nine months later, Laius kidnapped him from his wet nurse, bored a hole through each of his feet with a nail, and bound them together. Then he abandoned him on Mount Cithaeron. According to Willamowitz-Moellendorf (1919), both his parents took part in the abandonment after they had perforated his ankles and tied them together (just as one makes a hole between the tibia and the Achilles tendon and strings together the hind feet of a rabbit to make it easier to carry). Hence, at first the later incest is not the point at all. It lies completely in the background; the figure of the mother in Ranke-Graves's account is not involved at all but forms an intangible background, which carries an important significance for the theory of the year king who was sacrificed to the Great Mother. The central action is a pure power struggle between the two men, father and son, for rulership of the kingdom. Sophocles emphasizes this in his drama. In the first scene, it is said that Oedipus sent Creon to the oracle at Delphi to find out the means by which Thebes could be saved from the plague. Creon returns, bringing the god's word:

> The God commanded clearly: let someone
> punish with force this dead man's murderers.

(Oedipus the King, line 106f)

Here, too, there is no talk at all of incest or of punishment for the terrible transgression of this taboo; rather, the anger of the patriarchal god Apollo is directed against the father's murderers, an act that should be avenged in any case. The god's anger and the significance that is ascribed to patricide is understandable when we realize that Oedipus has unknowingly regressed into the matriarchal realm at a time in which the Greek patriarchate was just beginning to secure its position.

In the ancient matriarchal cultures as they are known, for example, from the Aphrodite Urania or the threefold moon goddess Artemis, the sacred kings who copulated with the Great Mother deities were killed and torn to pieces either immediately afterward or after a specified period of regency. At the same time, these sacred kings were always sons of the Great Mother. In the case of the Middle Eastern year kings, their body parts were then carried into the fields to fertilize them. The kings changed every year or every so-called "great year" (approximately every third year) while the Great Mother deities or their embodiments in the high priestesses remained and were understandably untouchable. The custom in the ancient system that the new king, although a stranger, was always the son of the old king whom he slew in order to marry his widow—for both were, after all, always children of the great Mother Goddess—was misunderstood in the later patriarchate and misinterpreted as patricide and incest.

Certainly by the time of Sophocles when the patriarchate was installed this misunderstanding was current. Nevertheless there is a noticeably matriarchal ring when, just before everything is revealed in the drama, Iocasta says to Oedipus:

> Why should man fear since chance is all in all
> for him, and he can clearly foreknow nothing?
> Best to live lightly, as one can, unthinkingly.
> As to your mother's marriage bed, —don't fear it.
> Before this, in dreams too, as well as oracles,
> many a man has lain with his own mother.
> But he to whom such things are nothing bears
> his life most easily.

(Oedipus the King, lines 977-984)

We know very little about the actual myth of King Oedipus. The story of Laius, Iocasta, and Oedipus was derived from a number of sacred images, according to Ranke-Graves (1960). One myth that could explain the name Labdakos ("aide with torches") has been lost. Ranke-Graves is of the opinion that this might refer to the arrival of a divine child who was proclaimed as the son of the Great Goddess. At the time of Sophocles, there must have been a story that the poet could assume was well known. Moreover, he could proceed with poetic license, in addition to which the text handed down to us is of a later date and we do not know the extent to which it diverges from the original. There are several Oedipus manuscripts that, according to Willamowitz-Moellendorf, all go back to a manuscript found in Byzantium at the beginning of the ninth century. This manuscript is supposed to have contained not a few alternative readings in which there were many errors and arbitrary interpretations.

Likewise, the ending of Oedipus—the touching picture of the blind beggar whom Athene receives and whom the dwellers of the underworld fetch into their realm—is surely a poetic invention. In the *Odyssey* and the *Iliad*, Homer maintains that Oedipus continued to rule in Thebes until he fell honorably in battle. According to Apollodoros and Hyginus, he was banished by Iocasta's brother, a member of the house of Cadmus, and pursued by the Furies. According to other accounts, Creon, Iocasata's brother, banished him after he himself had placed the curse on his sons, Eteocles and Polynices, that they would slay each other, which later did transpire. Likewise, the death of his sons was the consequence of a mutual power struggle for the regency, which continued into the next generation the destructive power complex occupying the foreground of the entire myth.

Therefore it seems to me completely legitimate to center the Oedipus myth neither solely nor primarily on the sexual incest complex and its consequences, as perhaps suited the attitude of the waning nineteenth century with its the sexual taboos, but rather first in a power struggle. At the oldest level, it does not even touch on sexuality but is concerned with the legitimate replacement of one year king by another, and only with the beginnings of patriarchy did it become a struggle of rival kings for regency, a bloody rivalry that continued for three generations. We might pause to ponder the extent to which this complex is constellated to a much greater extent than the incest wish and fear in our culture. I would not consider it legitimate to derive the one from the other on the basis of the historical roots mentioned here, although according to the Freudian theory, this would be a fundamental possibility.

The power complex is not only external, the rivalry between father and son or helpless child and powerful parents, but also—and for analysts more important—an inner reality with the same valence. The patriarchally structured consciousness of our culture carries on this power struggle against the compensatory matriarchal unconscious, which is devalued as an absolute bedlam of pure drives and desires that obey only the pleasure principle. If our violated inner nature does not avenge itself through illness, then at the very least we suffer a loss of soul and a deadening rigidity of personality, and to a great extent our ego becomes identical with aspects of the collective persona. From the beginning, and with some measure of success, Jung's analytical psychology strove to point out the prospective, creative, and constructive-compensatory possibilities contained in the archetypal structures of the unconscious.

Let us now take up the second point. Again and again, in contemporary analyses, we have the experience that it is not so much the fear of the punishing father that occupies the foreground of the psychodynamic processes but rather the much deeper and more profoundly unsettling anxiety of being devoured by the negative side of the maternal archetype. This is independent of the momentary flux of events and applies to both men and women. In our patriarchal culture, the ego-complex, be it a man's or a woman's, is initially identified with the archetype of the hero who, battling against the possessive, disintegrative, and regressive tendencies of the unconscious, must prevail and become stable. Erich Neumann (1949) pointed out that this fear of being devoured or killed by the mother, which finds expression in many mythologies and in the widest range of variations, is a much deeper anxiety for the masculine than the fears constellated in Oedipus. According to Neumann, this fear lay beneath the oedipal level and was uncovered only in the course of deeper-reaching analyses.

Since, as is well known, the unconscious relates compensatorily to consciousness, the development of consciousness must also have an influence on the forms of neurosis. We live in an age in which we are becoming ever more technologized at a fantastic pace and thereby becoming estranged from both inner and outer nature. How enormous these changes are becomes clear when we reflect on just the years of our own lives: in my childhood, a man who had traveled to Africa was a sensation for the entire neighborhood; only a few well-to-do people had a telephone, let alone a car; and civil air transportation was so much in its infancy that only a few crazy or half-crazy people traveled by planes. In those days, a trip from Berlin to Leipzig was an event more memorable than a vacation in Tahiti at Club Med today. All these processes cannot be without influence on the human psyche when we consider that we human beings are almost always uprooted from the stability of our birthplace (who today still lives where he or she was born?) and also fundamentally abandoned to an increasing isolation. It appears that the greater the mass of people that occupy this planet, so much more fragmented and nonbinding the relations between individuals become. In the post carriage or railway car, we still traveled together and could and did converse, while today in our automobiles each of us sits alone and isolated, making contact with others only through hand gestures from behind panes of glass. Nor is the modern jumbo jet a suitable place for human relationship and communication. The stronger this isolation becomes, the more intensely the compensatory, regressive longing in the unconscious must become to escape this alienation and to find our way back to the lap of great Mother Nature.

As I demonstrated in my book on the favorite fairy tale (Dieckmann 1983), a neurosis has a close relationship to a failed or not-yet overcome individual myth. This holds true for the Oedipus complex in psychoanalysis to the extent that an individual's emotional health depends on growing out of the infantile situation of this myth and overcoming it so as not to get stuck in one of the numerous variations of this complex. In my studies of the favorite fairy tale, two things became obvious: first, there was a great individual variety of different fairy-tale motifs that patients identified as being their favorite fairy tale from childhood and that depicted the central neurotic complex of each patient as well as the corresponding parallels in his or her psychic development and character structure with an absolutely incisive precision. Second, I found that these patients were all just the sorts of heroes who had not succeeded in solving the symbolic task the fairy tale set them. In a certain sense, they were attempting (unconsciously, of course) to live the life of their favorite fairy-tale hero, but often misunderstanding the symbolism and trying to live the symbolic concretely. In this context, I also pursued the question of the extent to which an individual is at all capable of freeing himself or herself from a personal myth or overcoming it, or to what extent the individual myth remains effective as an important dynamic background in the psyche, consciously recognized in its symbolic significance, which seems to me to be the case for many persons. As a rule, the kind of complex a person has tends to be less important for the individual's psychic health than whether or not the individual is able to deal with the complex, to experience it consciously, and to employ its archetypal dominants and energies at the appropriate and sensible times and places. I do not want to pursue this question further here, but rather turn our attention to the great individuality and variability of the mythological cores of the complex.

In my paper, "Die libidinöse Wiederbesetzung des Körpers in der Psychosomatik"* (Dieckmann 1981d), I describe two patients with the same symptoms. They suffered major anxieties of a partly phobic, partly hypochondriacal character, compulsive actions and ruminations, as well as depressive moods and feelings of inner emptiness and meaninglessness. Their psychosomatic symptoms differed only in that the one patient suf-

---

*"The libidinal recathexis of the body in psychosomatic illnesses."

fered from paroxysmal tachycardia while the other patient experienced excessive hand perspiration. Both patients had identical depressive-compulsive structures and could theoretically be subsumed under the identical Oedipal situation, if we ignore the fact that one was a man and the other a woman. But if we proceed from the point of view of Jung's analytical psychology which requires that we look for the individual background myth in each patient, it becomes clear very quickly that these two patients were fundamentally different.

In the foreground of both patients' consciousness was a mother complex experienced as positive, that is, both patients idealized their personal mothers and consciously had a very positive attitude toward them. The mythological background of the male patient corresponded, however, to the Attis-Cybele or Adgystis-Mythe type, while in the case of the woman patient a Kore-Demeter problem occupied the background. As a consequence of her tight symbiotic bond with her mother, this woman could not marry her Hades-animus.

Adgystis or Cybele is a great mother goddess of the Near East. Attis is her son, to whom she teaches the art of hunting and who, after he is grown, becomes her lover. One day, Attis falls in love with the daughter of Midas, King of Pessinus, and resolves to marry her. During the wedding celebration, Adgystis, enraged, appears with a lyre whose music drives the entire wedding assemblage to wild frenzy and madness. Attis castrates himself under a pine tree and then commits suicide. The figure of Attis is one of those youthful gods who do not yet possess the ability to separate from the Great Mother, to follow their own path, and, above all, are not capable of asserting themselves against the angry or negative mother. There is a series of youthful gods of this sort; among the best known we find Hyacinth, Adonis, and Narcissus. They represent an early stage in the development of the ego-complex in which it is not yet able to prevail against the unconscious matrix of drives and instincts and has not yet achieved sufficient ego stability to reject impulses arising from the unconscious. Attis belongs to the type that Neumann (1949) called "the strivers" who attempt to disobey the wishes of the Great Mother but are not yet able to fight for and follow their own way but are destroyed by her in her anger.

If one studies these myths more carefully and in greater depth and applies their images as well as their psychodynamics to the inner situation of a patient, it is often astonishingly convincing to what degree of detail one discovers the patient's psychodynamics in the structure of the myth. Myths are not only the first, pre-rational explanation and comprehension of the outer world surrounding humans but an explanation of psychodynamic processes of the inner world expressed in the universal language of images.

The imaginal thinking in the archetypal core of the complex indeed does not correspond to the secondary process thinking that is generally highly valued and holds sway in the sciences of our time. This primacy ultimately leads to impoverishment and desiccation and to a lack of real creativity, since new and different ideas and concepts can always arise from the magico-mythological depths into consciousness. Precisely in the realm of the psyche, we forgo of a multitude of fruitful possibilities when we are willing to renounce analogous, imaginal thought. If psychoanalysis were ready to include the other great mythologems that continue to live in the unconscious of our culture and could renounce conceptualizing the psyche exclusively under the primacy of the Oedipus complex, we would be able, in combination with the structures of psychoanalysis, to make fundamentally better statements concerning the inner world of our patients and the psychic illnesses from which they suffer.

It is the merit of psychoanalysis to have demonstrated the extent to which the individual's character development is dependent upon the process of socialization that he or she must experience. In the early days, psychoanalysis placed the accent predominantly on the personal father-mother-child triad in this process of character formation and left out of account the sociological constellation of the surrounding culture. As early as 1936, Fromm pointed out that father and mother were each only copies or representatives of the surrounding civilized groupings to the extent that they unconsciously and without examination incorporated the collective structures of consciousness and the corresponding values and ideologies and applied them in the rearing of their child. The investigations utilizing psychoanalytic insights that were undertaken later, especially by ethnologists, showed what significant differences in character from one sociological population to another can appear on the basis of differing approaches to early childhood rearing. Here we might at least mention Margaret Mead's (1935) fundamental studies.

The Oedipus complex is based on the model of the European nuclear family, and especially on the stern incest taboo that forbids sexuality between parents and children in our patriarchal European culture. Unjustifiably, Freud generalized this model to all human beings. Of course, this is understandable, for every child in every culture has a mother and a father, and for every child the mother, or the mothering person, is the first existentially important love object. What Freud did not take into consideration is the fact that the typical triangular constellation of father, mother, and child in other cultures is not effective in the form we experience it in our culture and that, in combination with other sorts of situations, there is a displacement of the incest taboo. Stein (1974) describes tribes of primal peoples who, in the developmental and maturational processes, experience the natural difference in age between parents and children as fully sufficient to exclude sexual attraction between the generations. For all practical purposes, there exists in these primal peoples no incest prohibition or taboo between the generations since mother or father are experienced as too old to have any sexual attraction for the child. Here the nurturing, oral libido is the only power that bonds mother and child, and the fantasy that "I will marry my mother when I am grown up" simply does not appear among these peoples, in contrast to our culture.

These cultures do, however, deal with the incest taboo between siblings much more sternly than we do. At a very early age, brothers and sisters are separated and reared in mutually exclusive groups. As much as sexuality among young people is, to some extent, uninhibited, it is strongly tabooed between siblings, something that is handled much more loosely in our culture and comes to pass more frequently than is generally known, as we know from our analytic material. Among these primal peoples, then, the psychically decisive and dominating element in development is not that of working through the Oedipus complex, but rather a complex that relates to the taboo against the naturally much closer endogenous sibling libido to be overcome to the benefit of a libidinally exogamous orientation. Hence it seems inappropriate to apply psychoanalytic insights to pathological cases in those societies, since culturally specific psychic contents are at work and other complexes are constellated in the ethnic unconscious. With its different course of development, we would be imposing contents unknown to it on a foreign culture.

From the very extensive literature on this topic, which constitutes the third and last of our objections to the Oedipus complex, I have mentioned only one example. Today, there are extensive analytic, ethnological, and philosophical investigations that distinctly question the general validity of the Oedipus complex, especially in relation to other cultures. Not long ago, a book appeared in Paris with the title *Anti-Oedipus* (Deleuze and Guattari 1974), in which—granted, again from an ideological perspective, this one Marxist—a multitude of these sorts of ethnological examples were collected which, for the most part, speak very convincingly against our being in a position to transfer this very specific, central European family complex to other cultures.

If the myth of King Oedipus is one of our culture's decisive complexes or, we might say, pipe dreams, then, in a better understanding of the power myths, we should conceptualize it as a warning. The person who believes he can become king over everything by solving a riddle ultimately ends a blind beggar while his sons slay each other.

Bibliography

Aigrisse, G. 1964. A Don Juan on the way to wisdom. *Journal of Analytical Psychology* 9/2:151–161.

Bach, J. 1972. Der archetypische Komplex "Seines Vaters Sohn." *Zeitschrift für Analytische Psychologie* 3/2:9–81 and 3/3:129–144.

Beebe, J. 1988. Comment on S. Ekstrom's paper. *Journal of Analytical Psychology* 33/4:345–350.

Blomeyer, R. 1971. Die Konstellierung der Gegenübertragung beim Auftauchen archetypischer Träume. Kasuistik. *Zeitschrift für Analytische Psychologie* 3/1:29–40.

Brockhkaus Enzyklopädie. 1975. vol. 18. Wiesbaden: Brockhaus.

Campbell, J. 1949. *The Hero with a Thousand Faces*. Princeton, N.J.: Princeton University Press, 1968.

Capra, F. 1982. *The Turning Point: Science, Society, and the Rising Culture*. New York: Bantam Books.

Chagall, M. 1960. *My Life*. New York: Orion Press.

Corbin, H. 1979. *Corpus spirituel et terre celeste*. Paris: Buchet and Chastel.

Deleuze, G., and F. Guattari. 1974. *Anti-Oedipus*. Frankfurt am Main: Suhrkamp.

Dieckmann, H. 1965. Integration processes of the ego-complex in dreams. *Journal of Analytical Psychology* 10/1:49–66.

_____. 1967. Das Lieblingsmärchen der Kindheit und seine Beziehung zu Neurose und Persönlichkeitsstruktur. *Praxis der Kinderpsychologie und Kinderpsychiatrie*.

_____. 1968. Das Lieblingsmärchen der Kindheit als therapeutischer Faktor in der Analyse. *Praxis der Kinderpsychologie und Kinderpsychiatrie*.

_____. 1971a. The favourite fairy tale of childhood. *Journal of Analytical Psychology* 16/1:18–30.

_____. 1971b. Symbols of active imagination. *Journal of Analytical Psychology* 16/2:127–140.

_____. 1971c. Die Konstellierung der Gegenübertragung beim Auftauchen archetypischer Träume. Untersuchungsmethoden und -ergebnisse. *Zeitschrift für Analytische Psychologie* 3/1:11–28.

_____. 1972. *Träume als Sprache der Seele.* Stuttgart: Bonz.

_____. 1973. Übertragung-Gegenübertragung-Beziehung. *Zeitschrift für Analytische Psychologie* 4/3:169–180.

_____. 1974. Das Lieblingsmärchen. *Praxis der Psychotherapie* 19/1:27–38.

_____. 1977a. Weiterentwicklung der Analytischen (Komplexen) Psychologie. In *Die Psychologie des 20. Jahrhunderts, Vol. 3: Freud und die Folgen.* Zürich: Kindler.

_____. 1977b. *Märchen und Symbole.* Stuttgart: Bonz.

_____. 1978a. Einige Aspekte zur Persönlichkeitsstruktur des Scuhtgefährdeten aus der Sicht der Analytischen Psychologie C. G. Jungs. In H. Dieckmann, ed., *Sucht als Symptom.* Stuttgart: Thieme.

_____. 1978b. Zur Methodik der Trauminterpretation. *Zeitschrift für Analytische Psychologie* 9/2:111–122.

_____. 1978c. *Sucht als Symptom. 2. wissenschaftliches Symposium.* Deutsche Hauptstelle Suchtgefaren, Bad Kissingen 1976. Stuttgart: Thieme.

_____. 1981a. Die Einstellung Rainer Maria Rilkes zu den Elternimagines. In H. Dieckmann, ed, *Archetypische Symbolik in der modernen Kunst.* Hildesheim: Gerstenberg.

_____. 1981b. Phasen des Individuationsprozesses in Leben Paul Gauguins. In *Archetypische Symbolik in der modernen Kunst.* Hildesheim: Gerstenberg.

_____. 1981c. Symbolentwicklung im Bildwerk Chagalls. In *Archetypische Symbolik in der modernen Kunst.* Hildesheim: Gerstenberg.

_____. 1981d. Die libidinöse Wiederbesetzung des Körpers in der Psychosomatik. *Zeitschrift für Analytische Psychologie* 12:269–285.

_____. 1983. *Gelebte Märchen.* Hildesheim: Gerstenberg.

_____. 1984. The enemy image. *Quadrant* 17/2:61–69.

_____. 1985. Die Bedeutung des Traum-Ichs in der Interpretation der Träume. *Praxis der Psychotherapie und der Psychosomatik.* 30:290–298. Berlin: Springer.

_____. 1986. Gedanken über den Begriff des "Feindbildes." *Zeitschrift für Analytische Psychologie* 17:25–37.

_____. 1987a. On the theory of complexes. In N. Schwartz-Salant and M. Stein, eds., *Archetypal Processes in Psychotherapy.* Wilmette, Ill.: Chiron Publications.

_____. 1987b. Struktur eines Komplexes. *Zeitschrift für Analytische Psychologie* 18/3:161–181.

_____. 1987c. Vortrag vor der psychotherapeutischen Gruppe über "den Komplexkern." Nürnberg.

_____. 1987d. Der Mensch und seine Angst. Vortrag im Südwestdeutschen Rundfunk.

_____. 1988. Formation of and dealing with symbols in borderline patients. In N. Schwartz-Salant and M. Stein, eds., *The Borderline Personality in Analysis*. Wilmette, Ill.: Chiron Publications.

_____. 1991. *Methods in Analytical Psychology: An Introduction*. Wilmette, Ill.: Chiron Publications.

Dieckmann, H., and A. Springer, eds. 1988. *Selbstzerstörung Weltzerstörung*. Olten: Walter.

Eliade, M. 1964. *Shamanism: Archaic Techniques of Ecstasy*. Willard Trask, trans. New York: Bolingen Foundation, Pantheon Books.

Französische Märchen. 1979. Düsseldorf Köln: Diederichs.

Frazer, J. 1913. *The Golden Bough. A Study in Magic and Religion*. Part V, vol. 1. London: The Macmillan Press, 1980.

Freud, S. 1953–74. *The Standard Edition of the Complete Psychological Works of Sigmund Freud*. James Strachey, trans. London: Hogarth Press.

Fromm, E. 1936. *Authorität und Familie*. Paris: Alcan.

Gordon, R. 1965. The concept of projective identification. *Journal of Analytical Psychology* 10/2:127–150.

Green, A. 1975. Analytiker, Symbolisierung und Abwesenheit im Rahmen der psychoanalytischen Situation. Über Veränderung der analytischen Praxis und Erfahrung. *Psyche* 29:503–541.

Grimm, J. 1945. *Grimms' Fairy Tales*. E. V. Lucas, Lucy Crane, and Marian Edwardes, trans. New York: Grosset and Dunlap.

Grof, S. 1983. *Topographie des Unbewussten*. Stuttgart: Klett-Cotta.

Harding, E. 1948. *Das Geheimnis der Seele*. Zürich: Rhein.

Hauff, W. 1896. *Sämtliche Werke*, vol. 4. Gera: Griesbach.

Hillman, J. 1979. *The Dream and the Underworld*. New York: Harper and Row.

Hoffmann, W. 1915. *Über den Einfluss der Gefühlsbetonung und einiger anderer Faktoren auf die Dauer und den Wechsel der Assoziationen*. Leipzig: Engelmann.

Jacobi, J. 1959. *Complex, Archetype, Symbol in the Psychology of C. G. Jung*. Ralph Mannheim, trans. New York: Pantheon Books.

_____. 1967. *The Way of Individuation*. R. F. C. Hull, trans. New York: Harcourt, Brace and World.

_____. 1962. *The Psychology of C. G. Jung: An Introduction*. Ralph Mannheim, trans. New Haven, Conn.: Yale University Press.

Jacobson, E. 1964. *The Self and the Object World*. New York: International Universities Press.

Jung, C. G. 1902/57. On the psychology and pathology of so-called occult phenomena. *C.W.* 1. Princeton, N.J.: Princeton University Press.

_____. 1906–1909/73. Studies in word association. *C.W.* 2.

_____. 1907/60. The psychology of dementia praecox. *C.W.* 3.

_____. 1911/60. A criticism of Bleuler's theory of schizophrenia. *C.W.* 3.

_____. 1912/56. *Symbols of Transformation*. *C.W.* 5.

_____. 1914/60. The content of the psychoses. *C.W.* 3.

_____.1919/60. On the problem of psychogenesis in mental disease. *C.W.* 3.

_____. 1934/53. The relations between the ego and the unconsicous. *C.W.* 7.

_____. 1939/50. Forward to Jacobi, *The Psychology of C. G. Jung*. *C.W.* 18.

_____. 1939/60. On the psychogenesis of schizophrenia. *C.W.* 3.

_____. 1946/54a. Analytical psychology and education. *C.W.* 17.

_____. 1946/54b. The psychology of the transference. *C.W.* 16.

_____. 1948/60a. A review of the complex theory. *C.W.* 8.

_____. 1948/60b. On psychic energy. *C.W.* 8.

_____. 1948/60c. The psychological foundation of belief in spirits. *C.W.* 8.

_____. 1952/53. *Psychology and Alchemy*. *C.W.* 12.

_____. 1954/59. Psychological aspects of the mother archetype. *C.W.* 9i.

_____. 1956/63. *Mysterium Coniunctionis*. *C.W.* 14.

_____. 1958/60. Schizophrenia. *C.W.* 3.

_____. 1959. *Aion*. C.W. 9ii.

_____. 1961. *Memories, Dreams, Reflections*. New York: Pantheon Books.

Jung, E. 1971. Der Grossinquisitor. Ein Beitrag zum Archetyp des grossen Vaters. *Zeitschrift für Analytische Psychologie* 2/2:79:104.

_____. 1973. Zur Gruppendynamik in einem Psychotherapeuten-Forschungsteam. *Zeitschrift für Analytische Psychologie* 43:193:210.

Kadinsky, D. 1964. *Die Entwicklung des Ich beim Kinde*. Bern: Huber.

Kast, V. 1980. *Das Assoziationsexperiment in der therapuetischen Praxis*. Stuttgart: Bonz.

_____. 1986. Die Bedeutung der Symbole im therapeutischen Prozess. In *Heilung und Wandlung. C. G. Jung und die Medizin*. Zürich: Artemis.

Kernberg, O. 1975. *Borderline Conditions and Pathological Narcissism*. New York: Jason Aronson.

Klein, M. 1946. Notes on some schizoid mechanisms. *International Journal of Psycho-Analysis* 27:99–110.

Kos, M., and B. Giermann. 1973. *Die verzauberte Familie. Ein psychologischer Zeichentest*. München: Reinhardt.

Kreitler, S. 1965. *Symbolschöpfung und Symbolerfassung*. München: E. Reinhardt.

Leonard, L. 1982. *The Wounded Woman: Healing the Father-Daughter Relationship*. Athens, Ohio: Swallow Press.

Lévi-Strauss, C. 1966. *The Savage Mind*. Chicago: University of Chicago Press.

Lévy-Bruhl, L. 1923. *Primitive Mentality*. A. Claire, trans. London: AMS Press, 1978.

Mahler, M. 1975. *The Psychological Birth of the Human Infant*. New York: Basic Books.

Mead, M. 1935. *Sex and Temperament in Three Primitive Societies*. London: Routledge and Kegan.

Meier, C. 1968. *Die Empirie des Bewusstseins*. Olten: Walter.

Miller, A. 1949. *Death of a Salesman*. New York: Viking Press.

Minden, G. von. 1988. *Der Bruchstück-Mensch*. München: Reinhardt.

Modell, A. 1963. Primitive object relations and the relationship to schizophrenia. *International Journal of Psycho-Analysis* 44:282f.

Neumann, E. 1949. *The Origins and History of Consciousness*. R. F. C. Hull, trans. Princeton, N.J.: Princeton University Press.

_____. 1955. *The Great Mother: An Analysis of the Archetype*. Ralph Mannheim, trans. New York: Pantheon Books.

_____. 1959/89. The experience of the unitary reality. In *The Place of Creation*. Eugene Rolfe, trans. Princeton, N.J.: Princeton University Press.

_____. 1963/73. *The Child: Structure and Dynamics of the Nascent Personality*. Ralph Mannheim, trans. London: Hodder and Stoughton.

Nietzsche, F. 1965. *Thus Spake Zarathustra*. Thomas Common, trans. New York: Thistle Press.

Pauli, W. 1955. *The Influence of Archetypal Images on the Formation of Scientific Theories of Kepler*. In W. Pauli and C. G. Jung, *The Interpretation of Nature and the Psyche*. New York: Pantheon Books.

Perera, S. 1986. *The Scapegoat Complex*: *Toward a Mythology of Shadow and Guilt*. Toronto: Inner City Books.

Die Psychologie des 20. Jahrhunderts. 1978. Vol. 7: *Piaget und die Folgen*. Zürich: Kindler.

Raffay, A. von. 1981. Der Salome-Komplex. *Zeitschrift für Analytische Psychologie* 12/3:227–254.

Ranke-Graves, R. von. 1960. *Griechische Mythologie*. Reinbeck: Rowohlt.

Rentrop, E. 1978. Der Messiaskomplex beim Puer aeternus. *Zeitschrift für Analytische Psychologie* 9/4:284–301.

Rhode-Dachser, C. 1972. *Das Borderline-Syndrom*. Bern: Huber.

Roscher, W. 1978. *Lexikon der griechischen und römischen Mythologie*. Hildesheim: Olms.

Sauerland, M. 1941. *Griechische Bildwerke*. Königstein im Taunus: Langewiesche.

Seifert, T. 1981. *Lebensperspektiven der Psychologie*. Olten: Walter.

Schepank, H. 1975. Diskordanzanalyse eineiger Zwillingspaare. *Zeitschrift für Psychosomatische Medizin und Psychoanalyse* 21:215–245.

Schwartz-Salant, N. 1986. Archetypal foundations of projective identification. In Mattoon, ed., *The Archetype of the Shadow in a Split World*. Einsiedeln: Daimon.

Stein, R. 1974. *Incest and Human Love*. Baltimore: Penguin.

Stevenson, R. 1979. *The Strange Case of Dr. Jekyll and Mr. Hyde*. New York: Penguin Books.

Theweleit, K. 1977. *Männerphantasieno*. Frankfurt am Main: Roter Stern.

Tolstoy, L. 1913. *Resurrection*. In *The Novels and Other Works of L. N. Tolstoi*. New York: Scribner's.

Velikowsky, I. 1982. *Das Kollektive Vergessen*. Frankfurt am Main: Ullstein.

Vincie, J. 1977. *C. G. Jung and Analytical Psychology*. New York: Garland.

von Franz, M.-L. 1992. *Psyche and Matter*. Boston: Shambhala Publications.

Werblowsky, Z. 1987. Religionspsychologiesche Aspekte des Symbols. Vortrag auf dem Wochenendseminar der DGAP in Irrsee/Allgäu, März 1987.

Whitmont, E. 1969. *The Symbolic Quest*. New York: Putnam and Sons.

Wickes, F. 1930. *The Inner World of Childhood*. New York: D. Appleton.

Wilke, H. 1977. Autoritätskomplex und autoritäre Persönlichkeitsstruktur. *Zeitschrift für Analytische Psychologie* 8/1:33–40.

_____. 1980. Der typologische Rahmen der Übertragungsdynamik. In Dieckmann, ed., *Übertragung und Gegenübertragung*. Hildesheim: Gerstenberg.

Willamowitz-Moellendorf, U. 1919. *Griechische Tragödie*. Vol. 1. Berlin: Weidmann.

Williams, M. 1963. The indivisibility of the personal and collective unconscious. *Journal of Analytical Psychology* 8/1:45–50.

_____. 1988. Reconstruction of an early seduction. In *Collected Papers*: *Through Paediatrics to Psychoanalysis*. London: Travistock.

Winnicott, D. 1958. *Through Paediatrics to Psycho-Analysis.* London: Tavistock Publishers.

Wollberg, A. 1968. Patterns of interaction in families in borderline patients. In Reiss, ed., *New Directions in Mental Health*. New York: Grune and Stratton